Table of Contents

Your Self, Your Esteem
Look in the Mirror

DUKE KING

TRIGGER WARNING: This book mentions and alludes to sensitive and possibly upsetting material that the reader might find disturbing and distressing, including, but not limited to, eating disorders, self-harm, substance abuse, and suicide. Please be aware of these and other possible triggers when reading and ask for help, if necessary, from the list of resources provided at the book's conclusion.

Introduction

"The universe works in mysterious ways,
but I'm starting to think it ain't working for me."—"Karma," by AJR
You come home from work or school and the first thing you do is stare in abject horror at the mirror in front of you. Your eyes become increasingly judgmental the longer you stare at the reflection, weary as they may be. Disparaging eyes glare in disgust at the view; all you can see are the many flaws that stare right back at you. They are roving in derision, critical in measurement, scathing to a fault. All that meets the eyes are blatant imperfections, and those insecurities overflow among the four walls of the bathroom. You stare, repulsed by thoughts yelling, "not enough,'" or the ones whispering that everything was too much to handle. There were at least 10 flaws to pick from a cursory glance focused solely on your face. You hate the very sight of your body, wishing you could change at least one thing to make you feel so much better.

Shaking your head, you try to ignore the roaring thoughts in your mind relentlessly and unrepentantly. Even then, you cannot help but take a few more glances in passing, even though you know how much it will hurt. You take in your appearance that seems horrifyingly ragged, and you cannot believe you went through the entire day like that. You begin to feel those tiny seeds of insecurities blossom just the slightest bit. With such thoughts in mind, you wrench your eyes from the mirror and plop onto your bed. The relief is palpable as you fiddle a bit in a grand search for your phone—your one guaranteed distraction from the thoughts and feelings flooding you.

Instantly, the refreshed feed is rife with pictures and videos of beautiful people dressed in gorgeous clothes and living what seem to be perfect lives. You cannot help but pinch your face and body as you stare helplessly at the images on the phone. That consummate visage, the golden ratio, the perfect life—all become so haunting and encompassing that those feelings of inadequacy and insecurities bloom in vivid colors. The little petals of insecurities begin to blow rampantly through your already unsettled mind, the whispers becoming war cries of self-deprecation. They turn into monstrous thoughts of hatred, as all you can focus on is how much the sight of your body disgusts you. You despise your body's mannerisms, its existence, and even your breathing. You wish you

5

had better looks, irrespective of the reassuring platitudes of others that you look perfect just as you are. They must be lies as there is no way you are as beautiful as they say. Your intrusive thoughts taunt you with a malicious remark: "All lies."

You start to lose confidence in yourself the longer you glance at the mirror and behold yourself in its glaze. Then nitpicking becomes a new ritual of sorts; its final form is a vicious cycle of self-loathing and envy for something you can never be. Eventually, the hatred becomes so all-encompassing that you lock yourself away from others, obsessing over something no one but you can see. Your self-esteem falls to an all-time low and leaves nothing but a husk of the person you once were.

Have you ever felt this way before? That haunting and crushing feeling of self-doubt and not being worthy of others' expectations? If you have, then know that you are not alone in this struggle. In this particular incident, feelings of dysmorphia run rampant, a condition through which a person becomes hypercritical of perceived flaws or imperfections that others often do not notice. An analysis by the International OCD Foundation reveals that body dysmorphic disorder affects 1.7% to 2.9% of the general population, which is about 1 in 50 people (Phillips, n.d.).

Many people may develop body dysmorphic disorder and are not inherently aware of it due to the associations and preconceived linkages with insecurities. Nevertheless, body dysmorphia is only one of the many ways a person may lose confidence and develop self-esteem issues, and the implications can be devastating. Viewing yourself in a wholly negative light spells out disastrous results for the individual and those around them. Maybe dysmorphia is not the cause of your feelings of self-deprecation; it can be the overwhelming pressures of societal expectations. It can be unwarranted feelings of guilt for things outside of your control. It can be the crushing weight of the feeling that you will never be enough; the means are endless and can be so overwhelming. Despite this, it is imperative to remember this: It is human to fail, doubt, and feel less than others. You are not any less of a human being than anyone else if you struggle with low self-esteem.

The age of social media and the reduction of social interactions bring a wave of self-esteem issues and problems. One of the primary issues is low self-esteem, which is now more prevalent than ever and is not limited to the angst-filled days of youth. Everyone is susceptible to developing low self-esteem, as it is no respecter of any person. There is no age limit, and it affects people of any demography or lifestyle. It is similar to weeds growing in your garden: You see them peeking out but ignore them, believing they will disappear or die on their own. Yet, you watch those tiny weeds proliferate and choke the delicate flowers growing in their rows with a horrifying realization. Low self-esteem is akin to this analogy. It comes unsuspectingly, presenting itself with signs. These warning signs are often unnoticeable or disregarded and tend to become more visible when the warning signs become too large to ignore or hide away.

A Safe Space

Nevertheless, within the words and characters in this book, there is a safe space for our readers, a place where you can rant and feel free to explore the nuances of your inner consciousness that can be so worryingly turbulent. Through this book, you can find a sense of acceptance and inspiration. Under no circumstances will your emotions be disparaged. Instead, the book is a place to validate your inner person; it is okay for you "to *not* feel okay." It is inherently human to fail, as only the divine is perfect. As such, the book's intention is not to chastise or condemn but to inspire and encourage a culture of self-love, validation, and confidence across the demographic. You are free to express your thoughts and opinions between these lines. Use it as a reminder that you, wherever you are, are more than valid, despite all the bad things that happen.

Your self-esteem matters. *You* matter.

Due to the sensitive topics to be explored in detail, please be mindful of potential triggers as you read this book. See within the references a list of resources that can help with queries about depression, anxiety, and suicidal thoughts. In addition, there are resources for medical care assistance for LGBTQ+ people and people of color—two of the most vulnerable groups of people dealing with low self-esteem, especially our youth. Our mental health is essential, and a list of resources is necessary for all.

The Importance of Self-Esteem Knowledge

What is the importance of knowing what self-esteem is? Self-esteem and its importance are necessary bits of information, especially in this day and age when human empathy is at an all-time low and people are more prone to developing low self-esteem. Self-esteem is not having an inflated sense of confidence and boasting. It is acknowledging your faults and looking beyond them to see your inner beauty and your true worth. Self-esteem comes from the ability to introspect and assess ourselves. It involves looking at the person staring back at you, acknowledging all the flaws and imperfections that come with your personality, and choosing to love those faults all the same. Sherie Newman puts this concept into better focus: "Liking ourselves and feeling capable are the foundations on which emotional health rests" (Newman, n.d.).

The importance of self-esteem, and thus knowledge about it, extends far beyond an individual basis. Information about the nuances of self-esteem enables others to be quicker in recognizing potential warning signs that can later become detrimental to their loved ones. Through this knowledge, people can become better support systems for those around them, especially those more susceptible to falling prey to the predator known as low self-esteem. Concurrently, knowledge surrounding the concepts of self-esteem means that you, the reader, become conscious of your subconsciousness and the implications low self-esteem can have for you. Low self-esteem can affect children, adolescents, and adults alike. No one is immune to becoming a victim of their minds. While self-esteem and its impacts are often difficult to process and acknowledge, it is a quintessential stage for that well-needed healing we desire. L'Oreal Paris states that we deserve happiness, good health, wealth, success, and love (L'Oreal Paris, 2022).

Above all, self-esteem knowledge implies that we can become more in tune with ourselves and become the best versions of ourselves. We can look in the mirror without flinching from the twisted imagery we judge ourselves to be. Instead, we can smile at the reflection, content with the person staring back, despite the sharp edges and blunted points we may possess. All those mishaps shaped the person you are now, and you deserve to be proud of having walked the wires and made it out alive at the other end. You are more than a conqueror for making it this far, and I hope you know this.

That is the reason to gain knowledge of self-esteem and, by extension, the premise of this book: to become the person we know we have the destiny for and learn that we are invaluable—we are human.

We are worth it all.

Chapter 1: Self-Esteem—What Is It?

"I deserve to be alright; I deserve to sleep at night. I'm my closest friend, I remind myself again. Better treat her well, 'cause she's with me 'till the end"—"Toxic Thoughts" by Faith Marie

Faith Marie details in her song "Toxic Thoughts" the spiraling thoughts of a perfectionist struggling with her toxic thoughts with lyrics reminiscent of a stream of consciousness. Marie speaks of her perceived inadequacy, anxiety surrounding her potential, and the crushing reality that we will not measure up to our expectations. It is an unsettling thought process rife within contemporary society, especially with the age of social media and changes in societal expectations. Our self-esteem still incurs much damage due to our perceived thoughts and biases, which are complex concepts to reconcile and correct. However, nothing is wholly impossible, no matter how daunting the task may appear.

We have established a few pointers on why self-esteem is so important. To better understand the intricacies of self-esteem, we will need to take a deep dive and first ponder the following questions: What is self-esteem? Is low self-esteem something inherently wrong? Will it only affect me in certain parts of my life? All these are essential questions that you may have—remember that no question is too dumb to answer—and this book seeks to answer all the questions you may have throughout the reading experience.

An Overview of Self-Esteem

Self-esteem is "[defined] as confidence and satisfaction in oneself" (Merriam-Webster, 1818d). The term is often stereotyped, boxed into neat little niches, and described as the personification of a person's 'ego' or 'pride,' which can be a potentially dangerous mindset. Words such as ego and pride, innocuous as they may be, have negative connotations that imply imagery associated with concepts such as a grandiose sense of self and conceit and thus referred to in a pessimistic light. Conversely, self-esteem should be seen as a state of self-respect and of realizing one's worth. That, in and of itself, is not erroneous; humans have the fatal flaw of compartmentalizing terminologies and form-fitting ideologies and concepts into restrictive areas. We tend to identify a scenario as solely black or white and designate it as such, even when the world exists in various shades of mottled gray.

Mind, which is a charity-based organization, supplements the concept of self-esteem by stating that self-esteem is the determined value and associated perceptions we have towards ourselves (Mind, 2019). As a result of our preconceived and often biased opinions of who we are, it is a difficult concept to radicalize. That is to say, our self-esteem and how we view ourselves are ideologies ingrained from childhood. It develops in an almost linear path, and it is a challenging endeavor to cast aside predetermined biases against ourselves and others. Quintessentially, we are usually stuck with these deep-seated biases developed from our interactions derived from external and internal factors.

Self-esteem spans three broad terms: low, healthy, and inflated. Inflation of self-esteem is a common denotation for what people often refer to as 'arrogant' or 'pretentious' and has negative connotations among the consensus, or what some may use about narcissism, which is a wholly different concept from self-esteem. Often described as wallowers of self-pity and self-deprecation, people with low self-esteem are ignored or disregarded. Such a thought process implies that people with low self-esteem pity themselves excessively and do not actively seek ways to improve themselves. Perhaps they are attention seekers. We tend to categorize similar-enough concepts with functions that have multiple layers. Think of it like an onion: The further you go, the more complex it gets, and the more you tear up. Due to our cognitive biases, we habitually merge similar concepts into a singular idea. Such a habit can do more harm than good and forces us to ignore things dangled right before us.

Similar to the differences between narcissism and self-esteem, a thin line exists regarding the concepts of "healthy self-esteem" and "inflated self-esteem." These lines, however, rely on others' perceptions and are uniquely based on our experiences in life. Such a statement means that where one person may see another as expressing their due self-love and intrinsic validation, another would chalk it up to the other being vain and self-centered. Such is the subjectivity of the terms 'self-esteem' and 'self-confidence.' Self-esteem is thus deeply entrenched in societal structures and constructs, along with the interpretations associated with each in tandem. Human behavior is an example of a social construct as it results from social interactions stemming from primary group interactions with family and close relations and secondary ones, such as colleagues in the workplace and peers in school (Moore, 2019).

Self-esteem levels, despite not being the 'end-all-be-all' method of determining our rates of success and achievement, and their impacts are far-reaching and affect multiple aspects of our lives. They encompass areas, such as our social life and ability to interact with others, the trials and tribulations of self-acceptance, and how we seek internal validation and love from ourselves in return. Self-esteem also impacts, but is not limited to, the following aspects (Mind, 2019):

- Liking and valuing yourself as a person
- Making decisions and asserting yourself
- Recognizing your strengths and positives
- Feeling able to try new or difficult things

As expected, the conceptualization of 'self-esteem' begins with the ideology of 'self.' The philosophy of the self is lengthy in discourse and extends beyond the general aspects of self-esteem. However, I will attempt to explain it as simply as possible and paraphrase where necessary.

The article "The True Self. Critique, Nature, and Method" (Sparby et al., 2019) emphasizes that there are many possible explanations as to what the 'self,' or as quoted from the journal, the "true self," is a reflection of the soul. The journal, citing literary and research works from scholars such as Baumeister and

Bushman, gives a diametrically opposing view of a person's self. The ideology of self is multifaceted and complex. Some annotated sources view the concept of self as being entrenched through divinity and a god's interference after death (Strohminger et al., 2017; Waage, 2008; Della Mirandola, 1996). Others remove the ideology of 'self' used in conjunction with the belief that it is a deviation from divinity. Conversely, the self is viewed as a culmination of human perseverance and is autonomous and under the dominion of the individual, far removed from the influence of God (Kant, 1968).

The article "Supplement to Self-Knowledge" gives an interesting take on the ideology and the intricacies associated with the concept of self (Gertler, 2021):

> In self-attributing a mental state, I recognize the state as mine in some sense, and my self-attribution partially consists in a reference to myself. This reference is reflexive, in that I think of myself as myself and not, e.g., as BG, or as the shortest person in the room. Nozick (1981) underscores the significance of being able to thus refer to oneself: "To be an I, a self, is to have the capacity for reflexive self-reference." This raises the question: How is it that I identify myself, and distinguish myself from others?

Self-attribution is "the cognitive phenomenon by which people attribute failures to situational factors and successes to dispositional factors" (Pompian, 2012/2015). Dispositional factors refer to causative behavioral attributes that rely on an individual's internal characteristics. In contrast, situational factors refer to features of behavior being the cause of situations or events outside of a person's control (Mcleod, 2012). Dispositional factors include personality, the propensity to trust, cognitive style, self-esteem, forgetfulness, and narcissism (Johnston et al., 2016), while situational factors rely on the context of the events observed as these factors differ accordingly. In this case, a potential situational factor for having low self-esteem would be dealing with bullies, a factor inherently out of the scope of the bullied person's control.

In essence, Gertler states that 'self' is no more than an amalgamation of what a person collectively ascribes to themselves and the scenarios that have made them who they are: a combination of external and internal factors. They made exciting viewpoints regarding the feasibility of a definition of self that prompts food for thought. They posit that the knowledge of self ultimately follows the principles of "reflexive self-reference," as quoted by Nozick (1981).

Self-reference, often depicted as an ouroboros (snake or dragon eating its tail), is defined as the act or an instance of referring or alluding to oneself or itself (Merriam-Webster, 1818e) and is the "[system that] collects information about its functioning, which, in turn, can influence that functioning," and is accounted for in social science through the concepts of self-fulfilling and self-defeating prophecies (Geyer, 2001). In this instance, the assumption is that there is a tendency to recall information better when linked to the self (Tickle, 2007), thus saying, "I broke the vase" rather than saying, "The vase broke." Consequently, we attribute scenarios and personality traits to ourselves to create a sense of who we are and what our 'self' may appear to be, rather than allocating said scenarios and personality traits to a more passive instance. Gertler raised these issues in light of this:

1. The distinguishing of individuals (i.e., the idea of self-attribution) and how distinguishing ourselves aids in creating our sense of identity.
2. Does self-awareness allow for greater yields of the material versus non-material nature of the self? These two aspects aid in the development of the 'self.' The material self consists of one's body, family relations, and possessions; thus, the concept of what is 'mine,' while the non-material self is the spiritual self that includes one's emotions and drives (Kihlstrom et al., 2021).
3. Does the ideology of self-awareness aid in conceptualizing a sense of identity in tandem?

The concept of self is far-reaching, challenging to explain expressly, and more confusing than helpful if navigated incorrectly. For this book, however, the main takeaway is that 'self' is an irrefutable part of what determines your esteem. Your morality is perceived and attributed to various factors but mainly by the situational and dispositional factors that may occur in your life. The statement implies that the self, and thus self-esteem, is the result of all instances and events that contribute to shaping our sense of identity and how behavior is observable. Low self-esteem is akin to a 'love-child' that is a mixture of our current mental health, esteem, and life experiences that assisted in shaping our personality and behavior.

Simply put, your self-esteem results from both nature (attributed to genetic disposition and biological factors) and nurture (the influence of external factors on behavior, such as life experiences and learning patterns). It depends on your definitive internal idiosyncrasies and interactions with the world around you (McLeod, 2018). Thus, *low self-esteem is a derivative of internal and external factors*. These factors have a long-lasting impact on our subconsciousness and affect our interactions with those around us. It can be the amalgamation of solely internalized or external factors but is more frequently a combination of both.

But what exactly is low self-esteem? Low self-esteem, as defined by WebMD, is when someone lacks confidence about who they are and what they can do, characterized by feelings of incompetency and inadequacy (Brennan, MD & WebMD Editorial Staff, 2020). Due to the implications of low self-esteem, there is a tendency to associate humble opinions of yourself with the concept of self-deprecation. But where does the line between self-deprecation and low self-esteem begin and end? Are the two one in the same? Or is low self-esteem far worse than the words we use to disparage ourselves and our values?

Low Self-Esteem: Is It Self-Deprecation or Something Far Worse?

The simple answer to this question is that self-esteem is worse than self-deprecation, but one is a true antecedent to the other and is, above all, linked intricately and seamlessly at times.

As previously stated, low self-esteem is associated with dissatisfaction and unhappiness toward your person, which frequently leads to self-hatred and destructive mental issues, including an increased risk of anxiety, stress, and depression, among other things. Dissatisfaction with oneself is not limited to just our perceptions of body image. It also includes gender dysphoria and our intrusive thoughts, or what some call it: our inner voice. Dissatisfaction extends to the feeling that we are not good enough, despite our achievements and the hyper-critical expectations placed on us. All of these can promote and encourage resentment towards ourselves and thus facilitate the emergence of low self-esteem. A person I know explains that low self-esteem makes them feel as though

> [I am the] most [worst] person to exist. You can't even look in the mirror without hating the person staring back at you. You feel too much, overthink, and feel like you *are not enough*. It is a vicious cycle, and I don't think I'll ever be able to escape it in this life.

The book *Self-Esteem: The puzzle of low self-regard,* stated this when referring to the idea of low self-esteem in correlation to self-concept, "which is defined as the culmination of our self-image, our ideal self, and our perceived value or self-worth" (De La Ossa, 2021). Baumeister (1993/2012, p. 4) stated this: "Low self-esteem individuals are, in fact, evaluatively neutral, and, more importantly, are characterized by high levels of uncertainty, instability, and inconsistency... People [with] low self-esteem have poorly defined self-concepts." They went on to iterate that people with low self-esteem issues tend to describe themselves with "middle-of-the-road" terminologies or undermine themselves.

Statistically, low self-esteem has become prevalent in all walks of society. The article "Relationship With Yourself" (Guttman Psy.D., 2019) states that an estimated 85% of adults and adolescents experience or have low self-esteem issues. According to DoSomething.org, 75% of girls with low self-esteem have reported engaging in self-harming activities in response to the perceived image of their body image and academic success (DoSomething.org, 2015).

Even a quick fiddling session on Google can show how a negative body image can fundamentally damage our perceptions. Curiosity led me to type in the search text "Why am I ugly" into Google Trends, leading to an anticipated conclusion. The search results displayed that across a total of 10 potential regions, five countries showed a value of over 50. These countries were the Philippines, Canada, the United Kingdom, the United States of America, and Australia, coming at value totals of 100, 59, 55, 54, and 53, respectively. Google Trends calculates their trends "on a scale from 0 to 100, where 100 is the location with the most popularity as a fraction of total searches in that location. A value of 50 indicates a location that is half as popular (Google Trends, 2022)." Such a statement means that in Australia, for example, the search text accounts for a minimum of half of the popular search terms used within the locale. It is a telling account of how deeply entrenched low body image is within the world and is not limited to a tiny section of the world.

Low self-esteem frequently harms your physical and mental health and your interpersonal relationships. Studies have correlated low self-esteem issues to eating disorders such as anorexia nervosa, bulimia nervosa, and body dysmorphic disorder and see these eating habits as a precursor to chronic low self-esteem (Silverstone, 1992). It has propagated incidences of alcohol and substance abuse due to the breakdown of feelings of self-care and love and the increased hopelessness and general apathy towards yourself.

Low self-esteem causes an increased risk of more intangible and just as damaging notions. It promotes and encourages incidences of perfectionism due to the perceived bias of being 'inferior' compared to their peers, persistent self-criticism, and self-harming behaviors such as self-mutilation or suicide (Better Health Channel, 2012). As a precursor of low self-esteem and a dangerous habit, self-deprecation is a commonly undermined trait among young people, with its adverse effects and influences on self-esteem often ignored.

When exploring the concept of self-deprecation, a song by Ezra Furman, "Take Off Your Sunglasses," stood out to me. Fulmer sings: "And then I woke up in the middle of the night, one night, and I felt so unworthy.... It didn't bother me too much, I think I am unworthy" (Ezra Fulmer & The Harpoons, 2008). Whether we like to admit it or not, we *all* have our moments when we feel as though we are unworthy or undeserving of who we are or what we have become. At times, we take an introspective glance into ourselves and are not wholly pleased with who stares back at us and use phrases or opinions that demerit us to make ourselves self-loathe a little less.

Self-deprecation, as defined by VeryWellMind.com, is the tendency to downplay your achievements or use insulting language towards yourself to appear humbler (Plumptre, 2021a). Often accompanied by phrases such as "Oh, anyone could do it" or "It wasn't any big deal," it invalidates the achievements and reduces the importance or value attached to the particular scenario.

We've all had instances where we downplay our achievements or make light of other aspects of our personality, such as saying our sense of humor is the result of our traumas or appearance, a tendency linking our physical appearance to a monster of sorts that has become so normalized that we are unaware of how intertwined it has become in everyday life. While self-deprecation is rooted in the much-appreciated concept of humility, it can lead to something entirely unwelcome: self-sabotage.

Self-sabotage has alternative definitions. One such description is that it is the active or passive measures we often subconsciously use that prevent us from reaching our defined goals (Jeffs, 2018), or it is the particularly destructive behavior of destroying or undermining something–in this case, our individuality, frequently in unsuspecting ways (MindTools.com, n.d.). Self-sabotaging comes in various forms and includes, but is not limited to, the following:

- Ambivalence: Within the context of behavior, ambivalence is the lack of the ability to make decisions or a general lack of certainty.

- Perfectionism: For this aspect, we are specifically focusing on the context of self-oriented and socially ascribed perfectionism. While perfectionism has its positive traits, self-oriented perfectionism means placing exceedingly high standards on yourself through intrinsic motivation; that is to say, you are attempting perfection for your own sake of validation. Socially ascribed perfectionism, however, is the conditional rise to the realms of perfectionism due to the cognitive bias that others—society—have high expectations of your actions. Only through perfection can you meet these expectations and thus causing validation and motivation to become extrinsic.

● Lackadaisical behaviors: Not giving your best.

● Taking on too much: Instances of chronic stress, burnout syndrome, and exhaustion.

● Being too nice without predetermined boundaries: Not learning to say 'No' or rarely, if ever, verbalizing and validating your emotions and opinions.

● Allodoxaphobia: This is the fear of opinions or criticism, often interpreted as unfavorable due to the formation of cognitive biases. A cognitive bias refers to systematic patterns associated with judgment and decision-making and is 'flawed' (Ramachandran et al., 2012/2012). They are inclinations not necessarily rooted in 'logic' but that are instead inclinations of intuition (Sala et al., 2021/2022) and are rooted in the concept of "subjective reality"—the perceived and often made-up realities that result from the individual's predefined biases that assist in forming a line of reasoning and logic. An example of cognitive bias is confirmation bias created through the tendency to consume information that aligns with, or confirms, our notions or beliefs rather than accounting for differing opinions or thought processes.

● Having limiting beliefs and an overall low self-concept and image.

● Feeling as though you are not worth anything, constant moments of self-doubt, subpar standards for yourself, or increased negative self-talk ("I'll never be good enough.").

The idea of self-deprecating humor has become a hallmark of what humor is, especially within the Gen-Z generation. It is an easy rhythm to fall into, but it is notoriously challenging to quit, as we tend to latch onto more negative implications than positive ones. It is, after all, easier to fall into vice.

The rhythms of self-deprecating humor are addictive, unassuming, and frequently veil negative emotions or opinions. An excellent example of self-deprecating humor is the joke, "Just because you are trash does not mean you can't achieve great things. It's trash *can* not, trash *cannot*." I remember watching a younger person I know laugh themselves into heaving breaths only to end with the blasé-toned, "Oh, mood."

Watching how easily we vacillate between finding humor and ruining our sense of perception makes for a horrifyingly remarkable experience. True to its essence, self-deprecation is not necessarily bad. Some may describe self-deprecation and its particular brand of humor as a covert means of manipulating people into thinking you are a humble person or as a way to not brag about your accomplishments around others. However, it is only relatively safe when used in moderation. As previously stated, excessive self-deprecation spells more harm than good for your mental health; anything in excess often spells 'danger' for our health.

Self-deprecation is often the precursor of self-sabotage and directly correlates to our self-esteem levels. Simply put, the more we self-deprecate, the greater the chances of us unintentionally sabotaging ourselves as we begin to verify the statements basing us as the true reflection of the 'self.' When self-deprecation becomes an integral part of who you are, when you are only laughing at the bitterness of your jokes, it becomes less humorous and thus more prone to self-hatred and low self-esteem issues.

In addition, self-deprecation contributes to an increased risk of depression and anxiety (Calmerry.com, 2021). Such a scenario occurs when you self-deprecate when you are alone, and where there is no need for jabs at your character or achievements. As previously stated, self-deprecation thus evolves into low self-esteem the more you believe in the punchlines of your self-abased jokes. Think of self-deprecation as you slowly chipping away at the core of yourself, steadily but subconsciously removing the bits and pieces of yourself that make you unique and wholly individualistic. You can also compare it to the story of the "Happy Prince," who offers so much of himself, yet receives nothing in return, leaving nothing but the husk of what he once was.

Self-deprecation, when used excessively, can do this to a person, much as it did to the Happy Prince. By constantly demeaning yourself, you lose sight of who you are until all you see is a mirror image you can't even begin to recognize. The concept of "self-fulfilling prophecy" lends itself here. A self-fulfilling prophecy is when an individual initially labels false statements as the truth until it ultimately causes them to become a reality (Jussim, 2019). In the case of self-deprecation, the flawed view of "I am not worthy" becomes repeated so consistently that you genuinely lack value that you eventually lose the drive and motivation to prove your worth. Thus, you fall prey to low self-esteem and lose sight of who you are. Furthermore, self-deprecation–and by extension, low self-esteem–affects you, the individual, and your interpersonal relationships as it causes a strain and disconnect between your perceived view of yourself and the perspective of those around you.

While teenagers and young adults are at an increased risk of developing low self-esteem, such is the cognitive bias, it is not limited to this particular demographic. Regardless of age, race, or gender, anyone can become a victim of low self-esteem. Such a statement, however, does not imply that since low self-esteem can affect anyone, every person's unique experience with low self-esteem can be invalidated. Conversely, low self-esteem appears in similar strains within different age groups but manages to have distinctive signs to be on the lookout for.

Low Self-Esteem—All the Stages in One's Life

Low self-esteem is not only a seemingly assumed "rite of passage" for teenagers, it is also a prevalent issue in all stages of life, with the premise of self-consciousness being a crucial precursor. The idea of self-esteem has had a history of being linked to teenage angst. Persons tend to write of teenage angst as a moody, idiotic phase all adolescents go through, but it is intense feelings of uncertainty and anxiety surrounding an unforeseeable future—a completely justified emotion, I believe.

However, low self-esteem is not a hallmark of adolescence; instead, it is evident among all strata of society and affects children and adults as horribly as it affects teenagers. Most self-esteem issues stem from childhood experiences that were not addressed and left to fester and grow malignant. Under this heading, we will explore low self-esteem through the eyes of a child, a teenager, and an adult.

If any of these experiences are relatable to your experiences or someone you know, it is advisable to consult a trusted person or seek the advice of a professional therapist.

Low Self-Esteem in Childhood

The age-old adage is that children live what they learn and that our collective childhood experiences can shape our adult lives much later. While this is not an undisputed or universally acknowledged truth, there are instances where the nurturing experiences in childhood had little to no impact on the adult's life, and the majority would agree that our interactions with others in that crucial developmental stage set the next stage for the adults we become.

In light of this, instances of low self-esteem in adolescents and adults can be traced to particular incidents in a person's childhood. Self-esteem generally emerges between the ages of four and eleven, as most social interactions have the most impact during this time (Ducharme, 2018). As such, we cultivate our sense of identity and awareness during this age, and incidents during this time often have enduring impacts on the remainder of our lives. A classic example is that a child bullied at a young age tends to develop low self-esteem and cannot overcome the traumas related to a particular phrase, action, or reaction.

A child's environment can have detrimental effects on their self-esteem later in life. High-pressure environments often have the opposite direction of our expectations. Instead of the child learning to be proud of their achievements, no matter how small they may seem, heavy pressures placed on children mean they focus more on trying to achieve perfectionism and the incessant feelings of challenge.

An article by Ishita Sharma, "Do confidence issues stem from your childhood?", states that a child is constantly surrounded by repetitive comparisons with their peers and their inclination is that they are only valuable as a result of their achievements often develop doubts of their worth, and they begin to believe that they are without value if they have no achievements (Sharma, 2021).

A child exposed to the conditional treatment of failure as unacceptable and something to be ashamed of creates a person afraid of failure and who seeks validation solely to obtain a false sense of worth and acceptance from others. Simply put, if a child is met with harsh criticism for the slightest of mistakes or reprimanded in an overly critical manner, this criticism only serves to promote feelings of self-doubt, hatred, and the flawed belief that they will never be good enough.

A colleague explained to me once that, as a child, they were often reprimanded and harshly scolded for making minor mistakes, and that scolding caused them to struggle later in their life to see their worth and view themselves as being more than enough:

> It starts small, you know. First, it is intentionally snide phrasing such as 'If you could get a 95, you could get a 100.' They'd seem pretty harmless, but this kind of invisible pressure forces itself on you. It makes you feel guilty for not living up to those expectations. Then it evolves into 'If person XYZ can do it, why can't you?' The stress becomes more tangible and feels suffocating with the need to strive for perfectionism. Those seemingly small, unrelated words snowballed together and caused me to constantly second guess myself. I found it hard to see failure as a normal process and saw it as unforgivable and disgraceful. I would have mental breakdowns at the mounting pressures and expectations and get ignored as I was 'overly sensitive.' I dealt with the guilt of not being enough by myself for a long time. Now, I'm pretty sure I'm depressed and anxiety-ridden.

Feelings of inadequacy from a young age often signal and perpetuate self-esteem issues and other mental illnesses in adolescents and adulthood. Additionally, due to a belief that their actions are irredeemable and need to be hidden, some children mask their emotions and feelings to cover up their perceived sense of failure. They may do so through increased acts of aggression towards adults and their peers, avoiding any activity that may highlight their imagined weaknesses, or the need for obtaining as much control as they feasibly can from others (Williamson, 2021).

Low Self-Esteem in Adolescence

Ah yes, this is the stage where people believe that we are at the most significant risk of developing low self-esteem issues. Technically, this belief is not incorrect. Adolescence is when we feel a tremendous sense of disconnect with ourselves and when we deal with some of the worst bits of uncertainty within life. It is an odd middle ground between hormones and confusion, as at this point, you are neither a child nor an adult. Due to this, teenagers and young adults are more susceptible to dealing with low self-esteem, primarily when a potential development of depression and anxiety is written off as "teenage angst."

At the root of low self-esteem in teens and young adults are the unchecked inner critic and the vicious cycle of uncertainty and regret of poor life decisions. MARINA puts this into better context with their song, "Teen Idle." In the song, MARINA laments her high school years, and this is a song of remorse for the empty reality hyped by the idolized teenage dream. One part stood out the most for me, encapsulating teenage remorse perfectly. MARINA sings in the bridge of her song:

> "I wish I wasn't such a narcissist.
> I wish I didn't really kiss the mirror when I'm on my own.
> Oh, God, I'm gonna die alone.
> Adolescence didn't make sense.
> A little loss of innocence.
> The ugly years of being a fool.
> Ain't youth meant to be beautiful?" (MARINA, 2012)

The juxtaposition between each line perfectly captures the vicious cycle of inner criticism and external ignorance that teenagers experience. The regrets that come with being both in line with what MARINA calls a teen 'idle,' an intentional mishap in place of 'idol,' yet being entirely yourself. While the years of teenagers are glorified to the high heavens, MARINA describes the age of adolescence as 'ugly,' and they are the years that push idiocy and the repercussions of said idiocy.

Through this cycle of self-doubt and instant regrets, there exists uncertainty and hesitancy to learn from those mistakes. It is easier to fall into a familiar rhythm of self-abasing and deprecation, and we become comfortable—better yet, accepting and blasé—with the cycle of self-doubt and uncertainty. Because of the unwillingness to try something that we believe will ultimately fail, we may be more inclined to avoid situations or opportunities for growth.

It may seem like a logical fallacy waiting to happen, but feelings of inadequacy may prompt us to not learn from mistakes. We may feel that nothing we do will ever be good enough, so why change the inevitable? Why bother learning from our actions if everything we do will have the same results?

Teenagers often have these thought patterns resulting from hyper-criticism, having their achievements undermined, and their failures blasted for all to see by their closest relations or caregivers. It perpetuates a cycle of waiting to change but lacking the necessary courage. It is potentially the result of a phobia of failure and the fear of the unknown. As teens—and even in adulthood—we often prefer to remain in our bubble of familiarity, that safe space we've grown to expect.

Adolescence is one of the most sensitive and vulnerable times in our lives. It's tough! Not only do we have the hormones rushing through our minds and bodies that make it difficult to think and process even on a good day, but we also have seemingly endless amounts of social pressure. We are more susceptible to the influences we are surrounded by, and, at this time, we are increasingly conflicted in deciding our shades of morality and consciousness that differ from the masses. Teens and young adults are at a crossroads at every turn and decision. They may question themselves and ask if they are to follow the road set for them earlier: *Should I follow my friend's vision, my family's, or something wholly mine?*

The pressures and expectations placed upon us in our teenage years can speak volumes for the person we become in our adult lives. Sometimes, as MARINA professed, we may even come to despise the person we became later in our lives. As such, it is of the utmost importance that the signs of self-esteem are quickly addressed during adolescence, as this can mean reducing the alarmingly increasing levels of teenage depression and of adults succumbing to depressive disorders and other mental complications.

But, as with everything, change and the drive to try new things is essential for overcoming low self-esteem and seeing ourselves in the best possible light. We can't do this if we remain rooted in our comfort zones. And, it is this comfort zone that may cause us to continue harmful or destructive habits. As the proverb says, "Familiarity breeds contempt," that is, once we've become so jaded and accustomed to our perceived bad habits and qualities, we lose respect for ourselves. The fear of change could be attributed to the cognitive bias of the "Status Quo Bias," which "refers to the preference to keep things in their current state, while regarding any type of change as a loss" (Master Class staff, 2022). Nevertheless, the first step toward self-confidence is regaining that sense of care and accepting our flaws, insecurities, and bad habits.

Low Self-Esteem in Adults

Low self-esteem in this stage of life may not be as widely explored and studied as in the childhood and adolescence stages, but it is equally as important. Due to the study of self-esteem and its associated issues being focused primarily on the preceding stages of childhood and adolescence, low self-esteem in adults is more of an umbrella term that captures all the aspects present during the two prior stages and focuses more on its linkage to depression and workplace limitations.

There are disagreements on whether teens who experienced low self-esteem eventually develop a higher sense of esteem the older they get. Some sources maintain that self-esteem levels are relatively stable and may increase during early adulthood (ACT for Youth Center of Excellence, 2003). Other sources give a linear timeline for this; for example, AARP.org states that self-esteem levels peak around 50-60 years of age and only decline after those golden years (Gibson, 2018).

However, as is the norm in nearly subjective topics such as this, individuals will argue that they feel worse in their older years due to the discrimination they face. One more senior person in the comment section of the article "Self-Esteem Peaks Around Age 60" explains her view on this take in the conversation tab of AARP.org's comment section (ef3487, personal communication, September 7, 2018):

> Very surprising to me to hear this since my experience is the exact opposite. I'm in that age group and my self-esteem is worse than it ever was. I feel unwanted by society and don't see much of a future.

In addition to this point, Masselink et al. stated that "[persons who have] lower levels of self-esteem than others at one time or point are likely to have lower self-esteem than others at the following time point as well." That is to say, while persons already predisposed to high self-esteem levels are generally resistant to developing low self-esteem in the latter part of their lives, others with a history or propensity to low self-esteem are more likely to have these issues in their adult lives. It is a rare occurrence for teens with high self-esteem levels to transition to adulthood and develop low self-esteem issues, as they would have previously developed an excellent sense of self-concept and image.

Low self-esteem in adults tends to be more nuanced than those in teens or children. Low self-esteem often emerges and becomes more evident in their relationships rather than being more obvious in typical teenage behaviors. The issue strains their ability to interact freely and efficiently with others, as they feel they are not worthy of affection or feel the attachment is not enough. As they indirectly seek love from their significant other, their methods of doing so may end with doing more harm than good, and they feel slighted, prompting a potential relationship deterioration.

In the article, "Low Self-Esteem Predicts Indirect Support Seeking and Its Relationship Consequences in Intimate Relationships," Don et al. (2018) state that individuals with low self-esteem attempt to protect their sense of esteem by using indirect means of obtaining the mental support and acceptance they need to overcome their self-stigmatization. It may also be a response to the unconscious desire not to be rejected by their loved ones. They may do so by clinging, whining, or sulking, which are actions often deemed as unwarranted and annoying when coming from adults.

Unfortunately, these actions may have opposite and adverse effects on their partners and can instead cause rejection from their partners. It can promote a sense of disconnect and perpetuates a cycle of adults with low self-esteem ending up in relationships with persons who may exacerbate the issue instead of soothing it.

Additionally, adults with low self-esteem may develop attachment-style issues. The *APA Dictionary of Psychology* defines attachment style as "the characteristic way people relate to others in intimate relationships, which is heavily influenced by self-worth and interpersonal trust" (APA Dictionary of Psychology, 2022a). They additionally state that the theory relies on the assumption that the degree of attachment is directly related to the bonds developed as children.

In essence, attachment style can be correlated to the bonds and attachments formed between the parent and child and can be a potential signal for the type of relationship individuals may end up in their adult life.

The article, "How Attachment Styles Affect Adult Relationships," clearly interprets these attachment styles and how they are formed (Weber, 2021).

There are four attachment styles recognized by most experts in the field: secure, avoidant, anxious, and disorganized. For adults with low self-esteem issues, disorganized attachment, alternatively known as fearful-avoidant, is more prevalent. Disorganized or disoriented attachment, as stated by Weber, arises from the sequelae left by childhood traumas, neglect, or abuse. Due to this, adults with this form of attachment find it hard to see their value as an individual or that they are undeserving of love and affection from others.

Chapter 2: The Many Faces of Low Self-Esteem

"Is that who I truly am? I truly do not have a chance. Tomorrow, I'll keep a beat and repeat yesterday's dance"—"Fairly Local" by Twenty-One Pilots

You may be noticing a pattern of alternative songs being constantly used so far throughout the book. There's a simple reason for this: Alternative music is one of those genres that truly sinks its teeth into the thought processes of persons in similar situations, providing a unique concept of what the chapter will be centered around. Plus, it is an opportunity to share some music recommendations. Once again, you are welcome.

"Fairly Local" (Twenty-One Pilots, 2015) is a song from the Twenty-One Pilots hit album, *Blurryface*. This is the personification of Tyler Joseph's (the lead singer for the duo) insecurities, doubts, and fears and culminates into one incorporeal and haunting voice that tells him that he'll never be good at what he does, no matter how noble his intentions are to help those in similar situations. In this particular song, Joseph sings that, despite wanting to make a substantial change in his life and his beloved fans' own lives by being a different voice from the dissenting ones they often hear, he realizes that he falls back into the same pattern of insecurities and doubts that he is trying to escape. He keeps moving with the sounds of the beat he is familiar with and repeats the same old dance of self-doubt and overly emotional outbursts.

Similarly, low self-esteem comes to us and sometimes seems to force us into repeating similar motions that we may be tired of but find it hard to extricate ourselves. Like the mire clay that pulls us down, low self-esteem often keeps us rooted in the fear that no matter what we do, the result will always remain the same, with no hint of change. After all, didn't Albert Einstein say, "Insanity is doing the same thing over again and expecting a different result"?

The survey says 'no,' but let us digress.

Those few words have a bitter truth regardless of who first said them. But within those words are limits we unconsciously place on ourselves because we are extorted that doing the same things repetitively means that we are insane, and we are less inclined to try and find new ways, whether to improve ourselves or otherwise. Yet, we may be surprised to find that low self-esteem and all its predictive factors are often unrelated but somehow seem similar.

Within this chapter, the focus will be on pinpointing the multifaceted nature of self-esteem and how it may manifest in our lives.

The Poster Children of Low Self-Esteem

In this context, the *Merriam-Webster Dictionary* defines a poster child as "a person having a public image that is identified with something such as a cause" (Merriam-Webster, 1818c). However, a poster child is not limited to a singular person; instead, it refers to any person, object, or situation uniquely identified with a cause or quality, especially in contemporary society.

In our case, our focus is on the poster children of low self-esteem. Simply put, it is answering the question of what low self-esteem appears to be. Many hallmarks of low self-esteem appear in various forms and misleading faces. As previously stated, these poster children can be more obscure than others and can affect anyone at any time, regardless of age, gender, or financial background. Inevitably, we are potential victims of low self-esteem.

The poster children of low self-esteem often align with the various complexes that float around, especially in popular culture. It may seem like a horrid pun that fell a little too flat—believe me, I am embarrassingly aware—the concept of complexes often implies the use of masking your feelings in a bid to cover up some perceived deficiency you think you have.

The Society of Analytic Psychology—paraphrased from Carl Jung's *Theory of Archetypes and Complexes*—defines complexes as "[being originated from] frequently a so-called trauma, an emotional shock or some such thing, that splits off a bit of the psyche" (West, 2015). The *APA Dictionary of Psychology* additionally defines a complex as "a group or system of related ideas or impulses that have a common emotional tone and exert a strong but usually unconscious influence on the individual's attitudes and behavior" (APA Dictionary of Psychology, 2022c).

Complexes may be viewed as an idealized defensive pattern resulting from physical or mental abuse, often casting shadows over the individual's psyche or the titularly named human soul (Hartman, 2015). Complexes typically develop during childhood and can have severe implications for an adult's attitude and behavioral patterns. Many complexes often disguise low self-esteem as something wholly differing. Still, we will only focus on the notorious superiority complex; the diametrically opposing, yet intricately linked, inferiority complex; and their lesser-known, but widely rampant cousin, the guilt complex.

Superiority complex, or what some inaccurately refer to as a "God complex," has made its due rounds around social media. It refers to, in colloquial terms, a person who believes themselves to be above others due to an overly inflated sense of self or who has an excessive amount of pride instilled in their bones. You could probably list a whole lot of celebrities who fit this bill. However, some other studies believe that the superiority complex is rooted in the concept of cripplingly low self-esteem and is only a deceptive mask used to hide this sense of low self-worth. It may seem a bit contradictory for a person to have low self-esteem and a superiority complex, but remember that humans are inherently contradictory at our core and that opposing ideologies can exist within a single person's particular brand of idiosyncrasies.

The theory, first coined by Alfred Adler, posits that in a world where persons struggle with a sense of inferiority, some may exaggerate their achievements to appear better in their contemporaries' eyes or even in their eyes. The superiority complex often does the opposite of its intended purposes as a defense mechanism to counteract feelings of low self-worth and confidence by using false bravado and achievements. It may make the person feel worse, reducing their sense of self even further. Hailey Shafir explains this ideology further (Barnes, 2021):

> Superiority complexes usually are defense mechanisms that come from deep personal insecurities, shame, and feelings of being inadequate in some way. Because shame is such a distressing and uncomfortable emotion, a person may use their defenses to hide these feelings from others, deny them in themselves, and avoid having to experience them.

WebMD characterizes a superiority complex as "a belief that your abilities or accomplishments are somehow dramatically better than other people's" (WebMD, 2021). Persons accused of having a superiority complex show signs of being what others call a "control freak," having an inflated sense of validation, believing themselves to be completely faultless, and emphasizing their achievements with no room for external validation.

Persons with this complex treat those around them condescendingly, undermine and demean their peers' accomplishments, and overly exaggerate their achievements in tandem (Barnes, 2021). The study, "Validation of Adlerian Inferiority (COMMPIN) and Superiority (SUCOMP) Complex Shortened Scales, places into perspective a few tenets of superiority complex, specifically the concepts of the supposed feeling of omnipotence, or the property of having unlimited power, in these persons. It states:

> [In reference to the study items] Items 5 (*Few people can compare with me.*) and 7 (*Normally no solution can be found without me.*) clearly presents the importance of the feeling of omnipotence in determining the existence of the superiority complex. Competitiveness and self-confidence are high load factors as well. (Čekrlija et al., 2017)

The article "What Is a Superiority Complex?" acknowledges that people have no direct influence or reason to develop this complex. Instead, they maintain that the superiority complex may be the Frankenstein monster of repeated failures. The article states that persons may learn and develop the habit of ignoring the elephant in the room by pretending to be above the issue or failures at hand (Holland, 2019). By feigning ignorance is bliss, they use a grandiose sense of being to control the anxieties associated with unsuccessful ventures and unachieved goals. Holland continues by listing a few symptoms related to the superiority complex. These include, but are not limited to, the following:

● High levels of entitlement and self-valuation.

● Propensity to grandiosity, or the "exaggerated sense of one's importance, power, knowledge, or identity—even with little evidence to support this" (Purse, 2022).

● A behavior pattern that lends itself to 'arrogance' and contempt towards others.

● Unwillingness to listen to others.

- Prone to mood swings, exacerbated by the contradiction of others.

- Underlying low self-esteem or feelings of inferiority.

The lesser-known link between low self-esteem and the superiority complex surrounds a singular concept. A superiority complex can stem from the expectations they believe are placed on them by their loved ones, and they hold steadfastly to the ideology that, to be loved unconditionally, the condition that they must always be better than others in all aspects must be fulfilled. It comes from a fear of abandonment and being left behind due to not fulfilling their perceived conditions. Low self-esteem comes from the fear and culmination of the notion that we are not good enough in the eyes of others. Simply put, a superiority complex is a form of low self-esteem that stems from the need for external validation and dealing with the consequences of that validation, whether it is good or bad.

On the opposite side of this spectrum is the inferiority complex. This complex refers to "a psychological sense of inferiority that is wholly or partly unconscious" (Encyclopedia Britannica, 2020). Also coined by early 20th-century psychologist Alfred Adler, an inferiority complex is the derivation of an individual's potentially perceived or existing deficiency (APA Dictionary of Psychology, 2022d). Persons who are said to have an inferiority complex often overcompensate for their believed lack of worth with excessive levels of aggression and experience a medical condition labeled as "chronic self-esteem." They are especially prone to self-deprecation, as they continuously view themselves as being less than others or having no worth to mention.

An inferiority complex is the near-constant imagery that, compared to others, we are worth nothing. However, it is worthwhile to note that feelings of inferiority can be seen as the standard. We will inevitably compare ourselves to our colleagues and peers, especially with those we believe are better than us in any particular aspect. Disappointment and frustration towards ourselves are admittedly normal functions, and it is perfectly healthy to feel such emotions. When we become consumed by the constant disappointments, and our frustrations turn into self-deprecation and self-hatred, the problem of an inferiority complex rears its head.

Many instances can lead to a person developing an inferiority complex. Often, it can be cultivated from a near-constant comparison and parallels drawn between the individual and others in similar age groups, socioeconomic backgrounds, or even gender.

A young woman, 22, expressed to me once that her sense of inferiority stemming from her dissatisfaction with her body image took root through her mother's 'teasing' words when she was in her early teens. She says:

> It was challenging to look at persons much slimmer than me and then at myself with any semblance of appreciation. I remember my mom teasing me that I was pushing towards 600 lbs. Mind you, I was already struggling with my weight and was a giant among my peers; no, the term was used with a more derogatory connotation than anything else. It hurt me a lot and only served to breed even more thoughts of inadequacy. I envied those who seemed effortlessly thinner and that made me push an agenda of skinny-people hatred. I would snort that most of them were dumb and that I at least had the intelligence to back up what I said and did. Yet, despite knowing that comparing myself to these girls would only do me more harm than good, I couldn't resist it. It was a horrible cycle of comparison, feeling inferior to those I deemed more beautiful than myself, and self-hatred. I still don't think I'll ever be able to rid myself of those feelings of inferiority in this lifetime.

This is a familiar reality for many who experience or may be diagnosed with an inferiority complex. This complex is akin to sinking under the waters, drowning in the murky waters of your emotions and perceived biases against your character. Persons who experience this often encounter significantly different emotions. Some become excessively timid, closing up on themselves much as forget-me-not does, while others hide these insecurities through increased competitiveness and aggression. Similar to how there is no one causative reason for an inferiority complex to develop, there is the general agreement that it stems primarily from childhood, but there are instances where the sense of inferiority develops in adulthood. An article by Elizabeth Plumptre, "What Is an Inferiority Complex?", explains that it is most likely an amalgamation of multiple factors that promote the growth of inferiorities within a person (Plumptre, 2021b). Such factors include:

- Childhood experiences: Some people would argue that this reason accounts for most of the feelings of inferiority that lead to the development of an inferiority complex. These complexes that developed from childhood experiences refer mainly to adverse events or circumstances that skew the person's emotional development later in life. Such cases could occur in high-pressure households, where the child is constantly made to feel as though their every action is never enough, and they grow up within this same mentality, unable to see their true worth.

Children who grew up in loveless households also latch onto this feeling of hopelessness and the belief that they are worth far less than others or are easily disregarded or abandoned. Inferiority complexes can also develop from children becoming excessively dependent on their parents or caregivers. A dependency personality disorder may develop through which the person feels as though they cannot do, or be, better without the explicit help of others and can feel as though they are nothing without others' help. Dependency personality disorder refers to an anxious personality disorder, with its victims having the overwhelming need for others to take care of them and believing they are incapable of making decisions on their own, as they are reliant on others physically and emotionally (Cleveland Clinic, 2017).

- Physical appearance: As stated previously, this factor can cause an extreme self-consciousness about our body image and can be the springboard into the deep dark ocean of the inferiority complex. This complex forces us to see our weight and physical features as something to hate or feel less confident about. Especially in this age of social media and the overstimulation of beautiful people, we view perceived flaws in an increasingly negative light, which prompts that feeling of inferiority to proliferate and spread unhindered within the subconscious. Chronic diseases can also increase the speed and development of an inferiority complex through self-stigmatization.

● Economic and social challenges: While these challenges manifest more during the adult stage, they can have severe implications for our mental health and propagate the development of inferiority complexes. Plumptre states that when an individual is deemed the least financially successful among their peers or has to seek assistance from their loved ones, it negatively impacts their self-worth. The urge to be economically independent is rooted deeply within us; thus, the stigma surrounding adults having to be dependent on others, regardless of extenuating circumstances, leaves a bitter taste in the mouth and promotes the feeling of worthlessness and uselessness. Feeling inferior can arise from differing aspects, such as the inability to obtain employment and failure to meet social expectations such as marriage and having kids.

The signs of the inferiority complex often overlap with those of the superiority complex, as psychologists have now deemed the complexes to be two sides of a different coin (Wisner, 2019). However, there are still signs to look out for yourself and others.

● Insecurity and low self-esteem

● Inability to reach your goals or feeling 'stuck

● The constant pulling away from family, friends, and colleagues in a bid to "fade away into the background."

● Sensitivity to criticism and a tendency to over-analyze and misinterpret compliments and criticism, with the latter frequently disregarded.

● A constant need for external validation from others, yet it is hard to accept genuine praises.

- May cause others to feel insecure in an attempt to mask their inferiorities and the avoidance of any activity that would showcase their weaknesses.

Additionally, there are signs of inferiority complexes that extend into the territory that others deem to be the hallmarks of over-confidence. These signs include, but are not limited to, the following:

- Excessive competitiveness: To mask their perceived inferiorities, people may use an unwarranted level of competitiveness to overcompensate.

- Perfectionism: As inferiority complexes result from the need to be loved by close relations, persons with an inferiority complex may become perfectionists to receive the conditional love they desperately desire. While overly confident persons get the attribute of being perfectionists, persons with an inferiority complex also face the issue of trying to be perfect but failing at every effort.

- Seeking attention: Persons with inferiority complexes may require those around them to focus solely on them, assuming their timidity is not a limiting factor. Seeking attention on the part of these individuals becomes a near necessity for them. They may feel that their efforts and worth are for naught without that sense of external validation.

Inferiority complexes and low self-esteem are often entwined and hard to differentiate one from the other. More psychologists see inferiority complexes as not a separate concept but as a markedly low sense of self-esteem. Regardless, our understanding of inferiority often restricts us from achieving the best version of ourselves. We can view this complex as the birthplace of our low self-esteem in certain aspects. The inferiority of self allows for the perspective that our image is far less than it truly is.

The guilt complex is the lesser-known, but inherently toxic cousin, of these complexes. As it implies, the guilt complex centers around the persistent and overshadowing sensation of guilt due to one's actions or situations outside of one's scope of control. Guilt complex refers to, as defined by Alderpedia.org, the expression and experience of feelings of guilt, usually in the context of severe judgments cast upon the individual of their own accord, viewed as a moral failure or unacceptable shortcomings (Griffith & Powers, 2007, p. 50). Kendra Cherry, in her article, "What Is a Guilt Complex?", defines the condition as the "persistent belief that you have done something wrong or that you will do something wrong" (Cherry, 2021).

While the connotation may seem inevitably negative, guilt is never an absolute evil. Instead, guilt is a necessary component of our emotional make-up. Guilt allows for the prospect of having introspection, or the "term is used in contemporary philosophy of mind, [which] is a means of learning about one's own currently ongoing, or perhaps very recently past, mental states or processes" (Schwitzgebel, 2010). It allows us to acknowledge our past mistakes and take the initiative of owning up to and correcting these mistakes.

Some would even attribute 'guilt' to the concept of our conscience, that little voice that often feels repentant after we've made our mistakes, although some people seem to lack this voice, which honestly explains a lot. Yet, as is the case for the previous two faces of low self-esteem, guilt in an excessive amount can have detrimental impacts. It can lead to a large wave of shame, with this excessive amount of shame potentially leading to extreme levels of low self-esteem.

GoodTherapy.org explains this in the post, "Therapy for Guilt," that explores the concept of overindulgence in guilt. They distinguish between guilt and shame first, as they both tend to be used interchangeably. The article defines guilt as "a sense of regret or responsibility that relates to actions taken," and defines shame as the "regret or sense of responsibility that relates to the self" (Types of Guilt, 2009). Admittedly, shame is harder to address as it is often more difficult to ascertain where the feelings of shame develop.

Guilt transitions into an excessive level of shame due to a person's conditioning to believe they were wronged by internal or external forces. Such a scenario occurs regardless of their direct or indirect involvement. Guilt can manifest itself in such a way that the person believes that they are inadequate in some shape or form. The guilt eats away at the rational and always prompts people to think that they are less than others due to their perceived inadequacies. In addition, this self-conscious evaluation brings along its old friends: feelings of failure, a negative perspective of self, and the existential dread that perpetuates guilt. You know that feeling and that confusion that leads you to question the validity of your existence and your purpose on Earth. Most persons experience existential dread at least once, often leading to a spiraling rabbit hole of self-deprecation and dissatisfaction.

Persons with a guilt complex have the immediate constant need to question the validity of their existence. Think of it as a domino effect: The person feels a pang of excessive guilt that morphs into shame. It extends into blaming themselves for situations decidedly out of their scope. Due to this imagined shame, persons may isolate themselves from others. Such a situation can lead to them engaging in behaviors that punish them for the supposedly wrong action (Cherry, 2021).

Kirby (2022) puts forward two potential theories for developing guilt complexes in the article, "What Is a Guilt Complex? And 5 Signs You Have One." The first theory posits that traditional psychologists view the guilt complex as behavior manifested and learned during our childhood. It further considers the implication of how incorrect connotations can cause this phenomenon. The psychologists argue that if guilt is viewed in an unhealthy or damaging light instead of a neutral and admittedly natural aspect of our psyche, then they associate the feeling of guilt with being something harmful or inherently wrong. Such a scenario may cause this emotion to become their default emotion, and they will have incidences of being able to feel nothing but guilt towards situations they have no control over or involvement in.

The second theory that contemporary psychologists offer is that, instead of childhood experiences, a guilt complex forms due to our cognitive activities. They posit that the negative emotion of guilt is linked with the tendency to misinterpret or over-generalize situations outside their intentions. Such an inclination lends itself to rendering the individual unable to rationalize their thoughts rationally. Their cognitive biases dictate that they are constantly in the wrong and act as such.

But what causes a guilt complex to occur? Just as self-esteem comes in myriad forms, so does the guilt complex Common types of guilt that lead to the complex include the following (Cherry, 2021):

- Natural guilt: This results from us genuinely committing a wrongful act and the remorse that occurs afterward. As previously stated, guilt is a normal response and an excellent means of promoting accountability and responsibility for our actions. We can learn valuable lessons from overcoming our guilty consciences and finding peace with our efforts. However, not addressing our guilt may cause vestiges to remain, which may persist for a long time and affect our mental health.

- Maladaptive guilt: The article, "Definition and measurement of guilt: Implications for clinical research and practice," defines maladaptive guilt as "[the] characterizations of guilt as a negative construct that leads to problematic outcomes. Maladaptive guilt involves processes that reduce motivation to engage in constructive behaviors" (Tilghman-Osborne et al., 2010). Another definition is that maladaptive guilt is exaggerated or misinterpreted, usually from guilt born from circumstances beyond one's control or when a situation becomes unamenable (Stuck, LCSW, 2021). Despise knowing the situation is beyond their control or that they are not to be blamed, feelings of shame, despair, and potential self-hatred can run rampant in their minds.

- Toxic guilt: Often categorized as a derivative of maladaptive guilt, this type of guilt generally accounts for the flawed perception that you are inherently an evil individual and constantly failing, or the idea that no matter what you try to achieve, you will ultimately always disappoint others because you are just not enough. It is brought on most frequently by self-judgment and a horrible sense of self-concept (Stuck, LCSW, 2021).

Various avenues can be utilized to create a guilt complex, with the case usually being that it is a horrible cocktail of multiple causatives, each with its brand of bitterness. These include, but are not limited to, the following:

- Childhood experiences: In the context of growing up in a guilt-tripping household, being constantly blamed for situations outside your scope, or being raised to believe your best is not good enough prompts an increase in guilt due to not meeting expectations. Guilt-tripping refers to a manipulation tactic used to imply that the situation at hand is somehow the other person's fault and plays on the emotions of others so that they (the person doing the guilt-tripping) are made happy by the other doing something to remedy the scenario (Raypole, 2020). A common one from caregivers is them listing all they have done for a child, so the least the child can do is perform whatever task the caregiver has given with minimal complaints, if any.

- Culture: This comes with the conflict of identity. A guilt complex can develop from the collision of values and norms differing from the ones you grew up with. Even if you no longer practice being a part of a particular culture, lingering guilt can propagate and cause you to feel ashamed for not acting in a certain way or not being proud of your history. The clash between the original cultural identity and the present one embraced can cause persons to lose track of what their identity truly is.

- Religion: Some religious traditions rely on feelings of guilt and, at times, shame to indicate to its believer that they are in the wrong. Most commonly referred to as the "Catholic Guilt," it is a prevalent issue, especially among younger converts in their adolescent stage. The guilt and shame manifest themselves mainly in teenage boys, who see God as less of a benevolent, all-loving father, but rather as a vengeful God, seeking to smite and bring punishment to sinners alike (Künkler et al., 2020, p. 11). The guilt complex forms as a result of the feelings of shame placed upon persons who have erred in the sight of God. It is an overwhelming feeling and tends to be judgmental. Guilt complexes formed from religion often play on the perceived guilty person over-compensating in their religious beliefs and may become extremely quick in chastising and guilting others to feel better about their sins, perpetuating a cycle of bitterness and guilt rather than the spirits of love, acceptance, and peace.

Guilt complexes are accompanied by physical and mental illnesses that affect their victims:

- Anxiety and depression
- Crying
- Insomnia
- Muscle tension and pain
- Social withdrawal
- Upset stomach
- Loss of interest
- Muscle pain
- Nausea
- Fatigue

Another item for this list is the preoccupation with past mistakes and regrets. This is evidenced by displaying an unwillingness to let go of the past and too often relive memories. Such a scenario is seen chiefly in those suffering from survivor's guilt. This refers to the "experience of feeling guilty for surviving a situation or experience that caused death or injury to others" (Lim, 2018).

As previously mentioned, there is nothing inherently wrong with guilt. It is a natural and secondary emotion that stems from the primary feeling of fear. Guilt can even become beneficial for us.

MindTools.com views guilt as a helpful emotion, as it can validate our morality and ethical actions and lends itself towards increased empathy (MindTools Content Team, 2018). Despite the unconscious inclination to assume that to feel guilty, you must feel ashamed, and these two emotions are not one in the same.

Some psychologists explain that guilt prompts a sense of regulation and restraint among persons, as it reminds us of the consequences of our actions (Stossel, 2020). Alternatively, shame is fueled by anger resulting from unchecked guilt and unresolved feelings of potential injustice. Shame causes us to lash out at others, not necessarily at guilt.

Nevertheless, coming to terms with unhealthy guilt is a step in the right direction. Understanding what is within your scope and accepting those that fall outside of your control can aid in tempering the guilt complex, primarily through the gradual process of learning that situations can and will fall outside of our control and that we are not bound to feel as though we are at fault for these things.

We've explored the ideology behind the different faces that self-esteem wears, much as a masquerader may change a mask. But what factors propel the development of low self-esteem? Is it one tangible source or a patchwork of multiple source fabric all sewn together to form a suffocating blanket of confidence issues and a lack of self-worth?

Factors Promoting Low Self-Esteem

Frequently, the causative lines of any reaction or action are blurred or tangled to the point of extremity, and we cannot find that one string to untangle the mess. Such is the case with low self-esteem. The factors that encourage or lead to low self-esteem are never clear-cut. They result from a causative action of another potentially unrelated factor. Knowing the potential risks and elements can help quickly address the problem or issue instead of letting it go unchecked and unaccounted for. Simply put, finding the root of the problem, while it does not guarantee a quick healing process, is always a solid step in becoming a better version of yourself.

Now, let's explore some risk factors. Two potential factors for developing low self-esteem correlate well and may be referred to when speaking of the other: dysfunctional metacognitions and rumination. Brooding, or rumination, in the far-reaching realms of psychology, alludes to comparing an individual's circumstances against a perceived, sometimes imagined, standard they cannot achieve (Gibb et al., 2011). Schneider and Brassen (2016) defines brooding as the express inclination to focus on the negative aspects of the negative interpretations we may draw due to our biases towards ourselves. Metacognition, however, refers to "the awareness and control of one's own cognition" (Baker et al., 1985/2010), or "the knowledge and regulation of one's own cognitive processes, which has been regarded as a critical component of creative thinking" (Jia et al., 2019).

As such, metacognitions refer to the self-awareness that comes with understanding our thought processes, senses, and experiences. LINCS.ed.gov gives excellent examples of metacognition, and the most intriguing one is that metacognitive activities include self-assessing and self-correcting, essentially known as self-evaluation (LINCS | Adult Education and Literacy, 2017). These allow for introspection, which prompts us to re-assess ourselves, what we have learned, and how we use external and internal stimuli to make informed decisions. As such, dysfunctional or maladaptive metacognitions may be defined as the impairment of our metacognitive activities by which our actions and self-awareness are negatively clouded by focusing on perceived faults in our cognition. Through this maladaptive behavior and resonance, we cannot view our efforts and worth in a positive light, leading to an increase in the potential risk of developing low self-esteem.

Hagen et al. (2020) examined the correlation between metacognition, brooding, and self-esteem and the symptomatic reactions of anxiety and depression in a journal article, "Protective and Vulnerability Factors in Self-Esteem: The Role of Metacognitions, Brooding, and Resilience." They maintain that brooding and dysfunctional metacognitions result from preservative thinking, which becomes a Shangri-la for developing low self-esteem. Perseverative thinking, or perseverative cognition, speaks to the repetitive and continuous inclination that focuses on the constant reflection on adverse events or scenarios. For example, the haunting thought that constantly reminds you of past mistakes is a beautiful example of perseverative thinking. It is a constant cycle that revolves and centers around the mind wandering to our mistakes. However, we dwell on it, not to learn, but to constantly berate ourselves.

Dwelling on our past, shortcomings, or flaws is proven to aid in developing self-esteem issues. It is human to think of our histories randomly and our weaknesses, as we tend to gravitate to negativity easier than we do to positivity. However, the problem begins when our thoughts become inevitably centralized on these unchangeable fixtures. As such, dysfunctional metacognitions and brooding reduce the chances of having a more positive outlook towards our future, accepting the past, and setting realistic expectations and standards based on our perceptions rather than those of others.

For the remaining and more commonly featured factors, low self-esteem, especially in teens and children, is a mismatched Frankenstein resulting in these experiences being predictive of future behavioral patterns and potential substance abuse. The following are possible root causes, as stated in the articles, "Tackling the Issue of Low Self-Esteem for Teens" and "Self-Esteem and Teenagers," (Galperin, 2018; Reach Out Australia, n.d.).

- Bullying: This is one of the most commonly denoted predictors and causes of low self-esteem. It can be seen as an extension of criticism. Bullying is a more vindictive version of criticism, which is not necessarily a horrible thing, but the connotations vary depending on the context. The focus is on tearing down another person to edify the bully, who may have insecurities of their own to hide. Bullies play on the emotions of their victims and frequently prey on their insecurities, plummeting the bullied person's esteem. Consistent attacks on a person, especially on a trait they have no control over, make for a near-perfect means of reducing a person's self-concept and self-esteem and are significantly exacerbated when done by a peer or someone in an adjacent age group.

• Chronic medical conditions: According to Pinquart (2012), the meta-analysis, "Self-esteem of children and adolescents with chronic illness: A meta-analysis," there is a potential indirect correlation between self-image, esteem, and a person's chronic ailments. The meta-analysis revealed that in the longitudinal cross-study, lower self-esteem levels were observable more in girls than boys, with a higher percentage being teenagers (Pinquart, 2012).

The article, "Persistent and Severely Mentally Ill Clients' Perceptions of Their Mental Illness," expounds on the potential reasoning for such an occurrence. It explains that chronically ill patients suffer from feelings of isolation or alienation due to their restrictive health accompanied by stigmatization associated with the illness (Vellenga & Christenson, 1994). Chronically ill patients may suffer from others' prejudices and discrimination of a mental, eating, or self-stigmatization disorder. A self-stigma is the internalized negative emotions one may have towards themselves due to their condition and the belief that their illness is an accurate reflection of their condition (Corrigan & Rao, 2012). Such a stigma commonly occurs in patients with schizophrenia who face a stigma from others and their own inner critic as they become subconsciously afraid of themselves or see themselves as dangerous.

• Parental criticism or neglect: Low self-esteem has deep roots in a person's history of extreme criticism. Hyper-criticism during a person's emotional and social development stages may have irredeemable impacts later in life. Such effects influence a person's ability to see their worth and constantly invalidate their achievements and person. Parental criticism can also lead to what social media loosely defines as "daddy/mommy issues." At the root of these is the excessive need for validation and attention from someone else, as their inner critic deems them unworthy of making that clarification on their own.

Neglect also has a part to play in low self-esteem. Negligence can maintain that sense of unworthiness the longer we go without the affections of those we care for or believe should care for us. Feelings of neglect can prompt persons to think that they are worthy of receiving the bare minimum of affection from others and are more likely to end with persons who push the narrative that they are unworthy or unlovable. Often, persons with a history of neglect end up falling into relationships that exacerbate their levels of low self-esteem and may even prolong that feeling.

• Religious beliefs and practices: These were previously mentioned under the concept of the guilt complex, but they are also relevant in explaining their linkage to the development of low self-esteem. This is not limited to Christianity, even if the more readily available referencing is the concept of Catholic guilt.

The article, "10 Sources of Low Self-Esteem," expounds on how religion propagates the occurrences of low self-esteem. Lachmann (2013) states that low self-esteem stems from the connotation that a belief system becomes akin to a disapproving or overly critical authoritative figure. They explain that this occurs when the believer has the deep-rooted fear that they are sinning, a situation that is a paradise for feelings of shame and suffocating guilt to develop. The stress of constantly living up to the standards of their religion, counteracted whenever they fail to do so by sinning or going against their believed divinity, the person can become confused and view their God as less of a loving Father and more of a merciless judge and avenger seeking to burn out the wicked. Such a scenario lends itself to the establishing of a guilt complex and the perceived feeling of being less than perfect, due to failing horribly in the sight of their religion or unworthy of their God's love. Through this scenario, they can develop an additional sense of inferiority and unworthiness, prompting a plummet in their confidence and esteem.

Factors that promote the development of low self-esteem are often either a culmination of past traumas that bleed into adulthood or issues that affect the older demographic more than they do their younger counterparts. With adults, the imagery is even less black and white, and low self-esteem can occur in the latter stages of one's life.

Relationships can often be a substantial driving force in the development of low self-esteem, due to an abusive relationship, the feeling that the individual is not enough due to their partner leaving them, or the constant comparison that leads to perseverative cognition.

In an article by Wisegeek.com, "What factors affect self-esteem in adults?", a user by the pseudonym of DDLJOHN explains their experience and their battle with low self-esteem. The reader/commenter states:

> I think relationships, particularly romantic relationships, can affect self-esteem to a large degree.
>
> I had very high self-esteem four years ago before I broke up with my boyfriend of three years. The breakup literally caused me to fall apart psychologically and lose self-esteem. I became withdrawn, I stopped meeting friends, and I stopped doing things I enjoy. I started to feel like a failure, like I was not worthy of good things. I basically fell into a depression...Before all this [the subsequent break-up], I did not think that a breakup could do so much to me. (DDLJOHN, personal communication, June 17, 2013)

In the adult form of low self-esteem, the issue can be the result of economic strain, specifically in the case of unemployment. A publication by Health.org.uk stated in their generated statistics that in January 2021, 43%

of unemployed people had poor mental health in comparison to those with employment (27%) and those on furlough or a leave of absence (34%) (Wilson & Finch, 2021). Such an onset results from the uncertainty of financial stability and job loss. Compounding this is the overall inability to see any sort of financial growth and security. Other factors that affect self-esteem include economics, relationships, and health issues. As previously stated, chronic illnesses, much as they would in a child or teen, promote the concept of low self-esteem in adults through the manifestation of self-stigmatization, which leaves a bitter taste in the mouths of its victims (Bargar, 2022).

We've seen the ways that self-esteem manifests itself. But are there any warning signs hinting at low self-esteem or potential red flags to put on a watch list? The simple answer is a resounding yes.

Predictive Thinking: Warning Signs

You may wonder, if low self-esteem is so apparent and evident, why is it so hard to spot? If there are all these factors to look out for, then identifying low self-esteem from its inception should be easy, right? Unfortunately, it is not. It is one thing to be aware of what causes low self-esteem, but its complexity increases when it comes down to the warning signs. The underlying problem with identifying red flags or warning signs is simple: Some people can seem to be very color-blind and can't see the glaringly red flag rushing toward them.

Despite that wording, the reality remains that some people can't see the problems at hand often since they have become conditioned to the situation, and it becomes difficult to address and correct the issue. Other times, these flags are written off as "fads" or the supposed way people try to get attention from others. Due to these misconceptions, we fail to notice these particular signs beforehand and only see them when the situation has blown widely out of proportion. Nevertheless, at the very least, it is imperative that we have a definitive understanding of these warning signs to help better ourselves or others who may be unknowingly going through this issue. The signs of low self-esteem in adults are similar to the ones found in children and adolescents, following a familiar beat of self-destruction and hatred.

Many would argue that early childhood is key to breaking the perpetuation of low self-esteem. The article, "What Is Early Childhood Development? A Guide to the Science (ECD 1.0)," determines that it "provides the building blocks for educational achievement, economic productivity, responsible citizenship, lifelong health, strong communities, and successful parenting of the next generation" (Center on the Developing Child | Harvard University, n.d.) Thus, many potential red flags indicate a child is on a collision course, with its destination being a one-way ticket to low self-esteem. Here are a couple of warning signs of possible increased risk of low self-esteem in children, as stated by Nemours Children's Health and AsTheyGrow.com (Lyness, 2018; Williamson, 2021):

- They become overly concerned about other people's opinions of them.

- They feel as though their efforts are less than those around them.

- They self-deprecate and call themselves with insulting language (yes, even a child can self-deprecate)

- They are hyper-critical of their actions and are highly doubtful of their abilities, yet find it challenging to accept both praises and criticism.

- They are overly concerned with how others view them and their achievements.

- They lack self-confidence and give up quickly as they fear failure.

Bring Me the Horizon, a British band known for its admittedly depressing songs has a piece called "Teardrops." A few first lines go as such: "[we] force-feed our fear until our hearts go numb. Addicted to a lonely kind of love." Despite others may write it off as an anthem for all the teenagers wallowing in their God-assigned right for angst, the song also spins the tale of a man, tired of hurting and feeling as though these unresolved traumas and fears are of more use when stuffed and locked away in his heart, forcing it to become just as jaded as he is. Many teens, or adults, have experiences like this or are currently doing so. However, signs of low self-esteem in teens take on a more dangerous personality, as there is the culmination of the symptoms previously ignored in the childhood stages. These indicators become glaringly red the older the teen becomes, accompanied by self-harming behaviors to feel better or numb the pain. Warning signs of low self-esteem in adolescents include:

- Self-destructive behaviors: These include cutting the body, excessive intake of substances that can lead to abuse later in life, and eating disorders due to a warped sense of body image and self-concept. That is, whether to believe they are too fat or have other bodily defects. Substance abuse may first occur as a means of coping with anxiety, but it eventually warps into the dependency of that seemingly happy rush and need to feel "Okay."

• Relationship troubles: They cannot form meaningful relationships with others because they believe the connection will eventually be broken off. Such an instance may signify an avoidant-resistant attachment style, which causes the person to avoid intimate relationships. If they can form relationships, the relationship may be too turbulent and complex to chart.

• Antisocial attitudes: This is a common sign many tend to ignore, subscribing to the narrative that it is only teenage angst rearing its head. Antisocial behavior makes its presence known when the teens sometimes willingly isolate themselves from their peers or close ones. They avoid new possibilities and opportunities to continue their comfortable routine due to a fear of failure resulting from past incidents and have difficulties making new friends. Additionally, they generally have apathy towards things that once motivated or interested them.

• Chronic negativity: This is a broad umbrella term and encapsulates feelings of unworthiness and the belief that they are unlovable, having a hostile inner critic that perpetuates those feelings of low self-esteem, or that promotes constant comparison to their peers, and the ability to take compliments seriously or without thinking they may a joke or lie.

In adults, these predictive signs have a few fluctuations that differ from the wavelengths of children and teenagers. Predictive symptoms in adults result from situations and experiences that occur in childhood or adolescence. However, as was previously highlighted, it is not so clear-cut, and the warning signs are not always indicative due to their prior experiences.

A surprising sign many overlook is low self-esteem correlating with the concept of dishonesty, which, in this case, is not limited to the baseline of pathological liars. Instead, it refers to the tendency of a person suffering and dealing with the burgeoning instances of low self-esteem to lie to not only ourselves but to our loved ones and those we surround ourselves with. The dishonesty stems from wanting to avoid the perceived consequences that may come with our failures or the confrontation of our emotional welfare.

Gilbertson (2010) explains that such scenarios occur when we find it is easier and less painful to lie about an uncomfortable event than to admit to the issue and confront it head-on. We would prefer to mislead ourselves and others that we feel okay, that it is nothing to be concerned about, as it is an easier pill to swallow than to admit that something is wrong or that we are genuinely not okay. Dishonesty removes accountability for actions, as the hallmark of honesty is the ability to take responsibility for our failures and achievements. Our reluctance to face the mirror image of our perceived faults in a truthful light promotes and encourages feelings of discontentment towards ourselves, feeding into the low self-esteem agenda.

If you have or know someone who has issues setting boundaries, there is a high risk for low self-esteem. Boundaries are often referred to in the physical sense. However, they are also a reference for the limitations or how far one person can intrude into another's "safe space." While confused with defense mechanisms, boundaries are not necessarily used for defending our mental stabilities and have the purpose of being a demarcation of what we are comfortable with. Due to our boundaries being reliant on our metacognition and experiences, the concept of boundaries is subjective as each person's boundary differs, and what is acceptable to one person may cause adverse reactions from another.

Gilbertson (2010) puts it as a divide between what's 'mine' and what's yours. They explain that they view it as the "understanding of where I end, and you begin." Poor boundaries do not incline solely on the perspective of one aspect. They encapsulate both loose and rigid boundaries, skirting on top of the extremities. As it suggests, loose or porous and rigid boundaries clash in their extremities and are each other's exact opposite. Flexible boundaries offer little to no distance between the initiator and the person in contact.

Persons who have loose boundaries are what is alluded to as being 'over-sharers.' They are characterized by the propensity to be people pleasers or find it difficult to say 'No' to others' requests. In the mainstream media, people call people who do so "Welcome Mats." It is particularly derogatory as it alludes to the person being only good for others to wipe off their dirty feet, but it carries the message well. They are additionally dependent on the validation of others. They are motivated solely based on receiving confirmation, accompanied by the fear of rejection, caused by the idea that if they do not comply with the demands of others, they will be inevitably left behind and abandoned. Such a scenario, unfortunately, means that these persons are at a greater risk of entering and accepting abuse from their significant others (TherapistAid.com, 2016).

Alternatively, persons with rigid boundaries are akin to an armed fortress, often impenetrable and difficult to overcome. They keep others at a distance as regards an emotional or physical space. Rigid boundaries are characterized by the tendency to keep their distance to avoid the potential sting of rejection (TherapistAid.com, 2016). Persons with this kind of boundary would rather spend the remainder of their eternity alone rather than experience what they deem inevitable. In addition, rigid boundaries prompt persons to come across as antisocial or exude antipathy, as they actively avoid intimacy, or if they do engage in it, they may come across as detached and distant. Due to their reluctance to engage with others, they are less likely to take the initiative to ask for help and may withhold personal information.

These particular types of boundaries result from the level of affection and care received in the development stage of a person but are not related to the attachment theory. Both boundary types are reflective of childhood experiences and potential traumas. For example, if the child is denied affection or feels as though they are invisible to those around them, they can either wear their hearts on their sleeves, leaving them vulnerable to the rigors and cruelty of the world, for the slightest chance they are accepted, despite their faults, and be genuinely loved. They actively seek the affection they missed as children, even though they know they might get hurt.

Alternatively, this feeling of neglect and rejection may prompt the child to close off, cave into themselves, or become prickly to those they deem a threat. They take their vulnerability and stash it away from the prying eyes of others. As such, they would rather be alone than give anyone the chance to hurt them again.

Through these poor boundaries of porosity and rigidity, low self-esteem becomes an overarching issue as neither boundary offers genuine assistance to keep persons within a healthy mental space. Both only provide extremities, and if there is anything we've learned repeatedly is that extremities give no help to our mental well-being. Poor boundaries are a breeding ground for insecurities, complexes, and the inherent ability to view yourself in the worst possible light.

How much control we deem ourselves to have can be a precursor to developing low self-esteem. We have the inherent need and desire to control something within the general scope of our lives. This could be what we wear, what we eat, or how we act. It may even extend into having control over someone else. While this may be acceptable in some circles, the idea of 'possession' is not without its negative connotations. Regardless, whenever we believe we lack control, it can affect our self-esteem. Here is where the concept of locus of control comes to play.

Coined by Julian B. Rotter in 1954, locus of control alludes to our perception regarding the amount of control over our actions. This contrasts this perception with the concept that our control relies upon the events we cause against external factors beyond us (Lopez-Garrido, 2020). This control is characterized by the internal conviction that posits that we are in perfect control of our lives and this accountability rests solely on our shoulders, and the external conviction that declares that life—and thereby our power over it—is limited by factors beyond our control or that we have no impact on the factors that may restrict us. In this sense, persons with a high internal conviction take accountability for their actions and all failures and achievements to their previous efforts. For example, they may say that they excelled due to their persistent hard work, and if failures occur, they have their shortcomings to acknowledge and improve. A high internal locus of control allows for more independent persons, willing to face the consequences of their actions, whether or not they are positive.

Conversely, a person with a high external conviction or locus of control believes that any occurrence in their lives results from external, often unavoidable, influences in their lives. Persons who resonate with this tend to underestimate their achievements and find solace in discrediting themselves. They may even blame others for their behavior instead of reconciling with the possibility that their actions also had a causative reaction. For these persons, any instance can be a potential avenue for blame, notwithstanding their involvement.

Not to be confused with the self-serving bias, a person with an internal locus takes accountability for all their actions, both successful and failures, rather than only attributing success to themselves and blaming external factors for their behaviors. Internal is active and external becomes partial to passivity. The *APA Dictionary* defines passivity as "a form of adaptation, or maladaptation, in which the individual adopts a pattern of submissiveness, dependence, and retreat into inaction" (APA Dictionary of Psychology, 2022e). As such, a passive person would have their dreams like everyone, but due to this maladaptation, the reluctance to take the initiative, and the inclination to inactivity, these dreams are unfulfilled, as that person refuses to accept that initiative, afraid of failure and rejection, and would instead become dependent on the frivolities of the world. They can become depressed as they suppress themselves and may develop an inferiority complex. It all comes full circle in human cognition's mental gymnastics.

Other warning signs of low self-esteem in adults are as explained by DoctorNDTV (2018):

- They are too critical about others, yet they cannot deal with criticism. This may seem oxymoronic, but hear me out. Despite not being able to take criticism aimed at their person or their ability, whether it is constructive or not, they are also critical of others. Some people may call this 'projecting,' as they may cast their insecurities onto others, using this to cover their problems. It may even extend into self-deprecation or the need to control their loved ones excessively.

- They may be quick to concede in arguments as people pleasers, which is a common characteristic among those with potential levels of low self-esteem. They put others' needs in front of their own to the point they lose sight of their persona or place others on a pedestal while ignoring their own needs and wants. They also tend to avoid arguments and conflicts and may even end up agreeing to ideologies they do not believe in. Such an instance reduces their presence and may prompt them to think their opinions are of no value, so there is no point in convincing others otherwise.

Of course, there will be outliers when referencing the intricacies of human cognition and behavior. Many of these signs, symptoms, and indicators can also be a precursor for personality disorders, mood disorders, or any other maladaptive behavior or disorder. As such, you must consult a trained professional to guide and aid you in correctly categorizing any potential warning signs you may have noticed.

You may have noticed I've constantly skirted around an especially prevalent source of low self-esteem in all walks of life. If you have, that's great! Here's a cookie for you. If you hadn't, that is also perfectly fine. Indeed, this particular source of perpetually dread and anxiety is now a seemingly inexhaustible source of fuel for the behemoth of a locomotive that low self-esteem is. We will now be exploring the tremendous impact and influence that societal expectations have placed on everyone, specifically in the new age of social media.

It is the click, after all.

But before that, can I ask you a question? To you, what is *your* self-worth?

Chapter 3: Social Expectations and the Media

"Being me can only mean feeling scared to breathe...When I wake up, I'm afraid somebody else might take my place"—"Afraid," by the Neighbourhood

The Theory of Self-Worth

Have you ever felt similar to the implications of the song? Felt the suffocating pressure of trying to fit in with your peers, despite the overwhelming suspicion that you do not belong there? It feels like you're a square trying to fit in a circle. It is ludicrous and painful, but you still yearn to be accepted by others. Have you ever felt afraid that you are dispensable and that somebody else will take your place with the slightest error (The Neighborhood, 2013)? It becomes harder to breathe, live, and exist without that existential thought that constantly questions our validity, purpose, and even the point of our existence.

If you do, know that you are not alone in this regard. Everyone, at some point in their lifespans, questions their purpose and despairs at the realization of their fragile mortality and morality. It is an inevitable aspect of human nature to seek out a purpose, as the validation of our purpose links with our self-worth. We associate our self-worth with our achievements and our failures. And quite frequently, our concept of self-worth becomes influenced by the societal expectations surrounding us. Our self-worth is a reflection of our self-esteem. If we have high regard for our worth as individuals, then our self-esteem would continue in this perceived tangent. Due to this, the hegemonies that are social media and their associated expectations—unrealistic as they may be—in turn, wield a heavy influence. Social media and expectations impact and, at times, impair our self-concept and perceptions of ourselves and, unfortunately, this can lead to us developing a train of thought with a final destination of self-hatred and low self-esteem.

Thus, we will explore the ideologies behind the concept 'self-worth,' which posits that self-worth declares that our highest priority is the search for a sense of acceptance of ourselves. Let's explore how our perceptions of self and worth become warped due to social expectations and social media.

In his speech, "Self-Worth Theory: The Key to Understanding & Overcoming Procrastination," Dominic Voge addresses students at Princeton University. Voge extols the significance of the self-worth theory of motivation to understand the complexities of procrastination, avoidance, and over-commitment. Vogue states, as transcribed from the YouTube video accessed courtesy of Tanya Cushman and Peter van de Ven:

[6:49] Voge: So self-worth theory asserts, or posits, first and foremost, that the paramount psychological need that all of us have is to be seen by ourselves and others as capable and competent and able.

[7:03] Voge: So in a school environment that means we need to be thought of as smart, as good at math if that's our identity, as the excellent writer bound for science. [Content Cut to timestamp 7:16]

[7:16] Voge: So self-worth theory says we need to be seen as capable and able and competent.

[7:22] Voge: That's what we need to do.

[7:24] Voge: And because it's the primary paramount need, we will actually sacrifice or trade-off other needs to realize or achieve or meet that need.

[7:34] Voge: And that's where procrastination comes in. [Content Cut to timestamp 7:42]

[7:42] Voge: Now, first I want to say that this is a model of people's beliefs about performance and ability, self-worth, and achievements.

[7:51] Voge: I'm not saying that this is how we should be; I'm saying that this is what we've discovered through research.

[7:57] Voge: Basically, we have this kind of simple model in our head that my performance determines my ability for the most part.

[8:07] Voge: Effort has a role in it, but ability, my innate capability and skill and knowledge—excuse me, not knowledge–my innate skill at doing something, largely unchanging, as that's what determines my achievement level, my success.

[8:22] Voge: And those achievements, those successes or not, determine my sense of self-worth, how I think about myself.

[8:29] Voge: So in a sense, then, these things become equated with one another. [Content Cut to timestamp 8:48]

[8:48] Voge: [referring to procrastinators and their thought process] Their performance is equal, or equivalent, to their ability, which is equal, or equivalent, to their worth, their self-worth as a person, as a human being.

[9:53] Voge: We used to think, in psychology, that if you really wanted to achieve, say, for success, then you would not automatically really want to avoid failure.

[10:01] Voge: But in fact, that's not the case. So not one dimension, one spectrum; there are actually two.

[10:06] Voge: You can approach a task, really want to do a task, and at the same time really not want to do a task.

[10:11] Voge: You can want to succeed on it; you can also really fear failing on such a task.

[10:16] Voge: So these are actually two different dimensions. [Content Cut to timestamp 10:27]

[10:27] Voge: We really, really want to achieve. It's very important to us; we're driven. Maybe you've heard that word used to describe you.

[10:35] Voge: But we're also fearful of failure and what it means. So we have two sources of motivation. So, in fact, procrastination, in many cases, and the cause of that is we're over motivated.

[10:50] Voge: We're overly striving both away and towards something. (Voge, 2017)

Vogue emphasizes a key takeaway through the 21-minute-long speech: Self-worth surrounds the ideology that our worth centers around not solely ourselves but in such a way that an external perspective views us as competent and able in our daily lifestyle. Vogue describes this as a "primary paramount need" in which we often sacrifice other essentials to actualize this perceived paramount need. Simply put, the need to prove ourselves can become so overwhelmingly chief in importance that we can lose sight of our other needs and wants.

During this book's writing stage, I asked a few of my family members to explain what they believed 'self-worth' is, as it was interesting to gain off-the-record insights into particular terminologies from those who do not have much interaction or interest in the topic. For the most part, their answers were in a similar form and ran in conjunction with the others.

To one person, their self-worth is "the value we place on ourselves, determined only by ourselves."

Another family member states that self-worth is what "you feel you are worth, your belief in yourself. It is determined by our achievements, and it means that we do not let others define who we are, and in essence being ourselves."

Another person believes our self-worth is our portrayal of others and ourselves; thus, to preserve this proposed characterization, we will not or wouldn't act on situations that would diminish our sense of self-worth. They added that achievements are not the end all be all of what determines our self-worth; instead, they state that those around us help to create and solidify this ideology and imagery surrounded by self-worth.

The University of North Carolina Wilmington (UNCW) defines self-worth as "the internal sense of being good enough and worthy of love and belonging from others" (UNCW, n.d.). The *APA Dictionary of Psychology* proposes a similar definition for the ideology of self-worth. It states that self-worth is "an individual's evaluation of himself or herself as a valuable, capable human being deserving of respect and consideration" (APA Dictionary of Psychology, 2022f). As such, self-worth, as previously established, centers on the chief concept that it is reliant on one's self and evaluation to assign themselves as a capable human being.

While the arbitrary definition links 'self-worth' as a synonym of 'self-esteem,' they are not the same. Gooden, Ph.D. (2020) offers a distinction between the two similar concepts:

> Our self-esteem is derived from our abilities, accomplishments, social positions, and things we believe and we can achieve. We can bolster our self-esteem by improving our skills or performance, and our self-esteem goes up and down depending on how we're doing in various aspects of our lives.
>
> In contrast, unconditional self-worth is distinct from our abilities and accomplishments. It's not about comparing ourselves to others; it's not something that we can have more or less of. Unconditional self-worth is the sense that you deserve to be alive, to be loved and cared for."

In layman's terms, self-esteem develops from external validation and fluctuates depending on our actions' reception from others. This increases when our achievements are praised but sinks on the premise of our failures. Alternatively, self-worth should be from introspection, bolstered by, but not limited to, our accomplishments and failures. Thus the theory of self-worth is born. It is the inherent ability to view ourselves as deserving of love, affection, and respect.

Thus lies the ideology behind the self-worth theory. The theory of self-worth, introduced by Covington and Beery in 1976, posits that our self-worth, our chief goal, is the usual self-acceptance. We develop this sense of self-acceptance, or our embracing of all attributes, whether positive or negative (Virginia Department of Health, n.d.), through achievements crafted through competition and the associated merits gained (Ackerman, MA., 2018).

The theory continues by attributing four vital elements to the successful development of the self-worth model: ability, effort, performance, and self-worth. Ability and effort have significant ramifications and influence our performance, which, in turn, prompts an increase in our self-worth. However, self-worth is not limited solely to achievement. Instead, our sense of self-worth culminates from different yardsticks for measurements: our perception of beauty, materialism (i.e., inclusive of net incomes and possessions), and our position in society. Yet, these yardsticks still seem to link with the overarching idea of achievements.

As stated earlier, self-worth should rely on the merits of self-acceptance and general happiness with the person we have become. However, the operative word here is *should*. Excessive attribution has led to a skewing of the basis of self-worth. Due to the heavy emphasis on achievements, we have now come to entirely base our perceived value as human beings on our achievements, and these become the very building blocks of our self-worth. Rather than being the result of self-acceptance, our self-worth is now reliant on our thresholds of achievement, which means that with the absence of solid accomplishments, our self-worth is biased, and we are led to believe there is no value to an individual without any semblance of achievement.

Schools tend to give the impression that our achievements are the only means of measuring our worth, which often causes more adverse reactions in students rather than being a means of encouragement. That is understandable. By allowing the thought process of using achievement to be the most significant threshold, there is the underlying implication floating around that devalues and reduces our multifaceted existence to solely what is achievable.

Achievement is not the same as an ability or the same as self-worth. It is only a facet of both terms and a necessary one, but it must not be the hallmark for our level of self-worth. Doing so can invalidate our individuality and raise the risk of low self-esteem due to this invalidation.

Humans have an inescapable mindset that focuses solely on the concept of 'ability' that precedes 'achievements.' However, we ignore the core concept of 'effort' when we do so. Effort is a necessary aspect that develops self-worth, as it is the motivational force that prompts us to act in a way that will promote our sense of achievement and self-worth.

However, neither effort nor ability is mutually inclusive, and both can exist without the other. For example, let's say you have excellent painting skills and entered an art competition, with recognition, praise, and monetary fulfillment being the reward for your hard work.

But you failed to put in the required effort to complete the task, thus reducing your performance and losing that sense of achievement that comes with making a successful piece.

Alternatively, you may put in much effort into an art piece, but your lack of ability or talent created a dent in your achievements. Despite this, I am not trying to say that you can't achieve solely on the merit of effort or ability, but let me leave this food for thought: Can we subsist purely on one aspect for the remainder of our lives? We can only do so much through sheer perseverance and effort. In the same breath, how far can raw talent and ability carry us before we lose that inspiration and vision that allowed this ability to manifest?

Regardless, the concept behind ability and effort and their perceived impacts depends entirely on the individual. It is not necessarily a derivative of external or situational factors affecting our performance, our achievements, and thus our self-worth. Realizing that our self-worth is not reliant on the validation or rejection of others and that it is the complex process of self-acceptance, as we would have already taken the first step to developing a higher sense of self-worth and, by extension, of self-esteem.

Gooden (2020) in her article, "How to cultivate a sense of unconditional self-worth," explains to her readers the struggles she faced due to the implications and the multiple hits she took. In her younger years, Gooden believed that, if she threw herself into the pursuit of perfectionism and achievements, her efforts fill the void of worthlessness. Gooden states:

> So, at around the age of 12, I decided that the way to cure these feelings of unworthiness was perfection. Simple, right? If I was just perfect, then I would fit in. I would be chosen. I would really be happy.
>
> I threw myself into formal dance classes, worked hard in school and tried to be a supportive and selfless friend. My self-esteem was high when I got good grades and felt included—but it crashed when I didn't do well academically or was left out.
>
> In college, busyness became my key strategy for trying to feel worthy. I juggled classes and tutoring with the Black Student Union, student government, gospel choir, step team... I barely gave myself time to breathe, to think, to be.

After college, my attention turned to trying to find a relationship to feel the void. The anxiety and ups and downs I experienced in this quest were exhausting. I remember going out to bars and clubs, and just like in junior high, I was rarely the one chosen to dance. I began to question my attractiveness with my brown skin and kinky hair and whether I'd ever be accepted by a potential partner. I held on to the hope that if I could just find someone to love me, then I would finally feel worthy.

Such a personal story may resonate with you and is common among persons who suffer from low levels of self-worth. While her experience may be more racially motivated, it does not detract from the relevance and implications of her story.

Regardless of our race, age, and gender preferences or how we identify sexually, all of us have felt that unpleasant sensation of worthlessness. We feel as though we are not enough, and to prove to others—and less to ourselves—that we are more than enough as we overcompensate. Yet, this overcompensation often leaves us emptier than we were before, and in the same breath, we feel so much more exhausted and unfulfilled. Some psychologists view this overcompensation as a defense mechanism to prevent us from getting hurt or losing the sense of satisfaction and acceptance from others rather than from ourselves.

The article "What's your coping mode: Surrender, avoidance, or overcompensation?" highlights overcompensation as a defense and coping mechanism. Overcompensation may be the antithesis of our predefined schemata, used as a cover-up for what we believe is our inadequacies. *The APA Dictionary* refers to overcompensation through its root word, 'compensation.' They allude to compensation as the "substitution or development of strength or capability in one area to offset real or imagined deficiency in another...Overcompensation [is] when the substitute behavior exceeds what might actually be necessary in terms of level of compensation for the deficiency" (APA Dictionary of Psychology, 2022b)."

The Encyclopedia Britannica adds to this definition by stating that schemata are the "mental structures that an individual uses to organize knowledge and guide cognitive processes and behavior" (Michalak, 2019). As such, our overcompensation of attitudes, behavioral patterns, and worth could very well be a defensive coping mechanism used to hide from others, even ourselves, unsurprisingly and display a persona that may be wholly unlike the realistic reflections of ourselves.

Van der Linden's (2016) article "What's your coping mode: Surrender, avoidant or overcompensation?" proposes that we use overcompensation when we act in a way that is opposite to how cognition makes us feel. In the case of Gooden, her method for gaining self-worth was not accepting her shortcomings, accepting who she is, or celebrating the small things that make her individual and unique. Instead, she hides her insecurities and pushes herself to the realms of physical, emotional, and mental exhaustion, believing that doing so will make her feel better about her perceived weaknesses.

The article explains that overcompensation prompts behaviors or patterns that do not reflect our actual nature or personality but a persona that allows us to act in such a way we never would initially and one that compensates for our unmet needs (Van der Linden, 2016).

In a letter to his brother, Theo, Vincent van Gogh said, "If you hear a voice within you say 'you cannot paint,' then by all means paint, and that voice will be silenced (circa 1883)." This is valuable advice, but there are times when our doubts are so encompassing that instead of these choices becoming silent as we attempt what we believe we cannot do, they become louder in their pitch, especially in our failures. What we face here is 'self-doubt' that develops through what is presumed to be repeated failures, defined as "a state of uncertainty about the truth of anything...[such as] our thoughts, beliefs, emotions, opinions, decisions, self-views, or any 'truth' we hold in our minds" (Davis, n.d.).

Our self-doubt inclines us more to our concept of competence. It prompts us to question our abilities and question whether we are as good as we previously believed. As a result, we examine and challenge our perceived level of competency, which links with our sense of achievement. Due to this re-evaluation and the constant doubt that plagues our achievements, we begin to lessen our initial assessment of self-worth. As we struggle with this decrease in self-worth, our self-perception and esteem also get damaged.

In the wise words of Kronk from the movie *The Emperor's New Groove*: "It's all coming together."

However, as with every instance, not everyone experiences self-worth or self-worth in similar strains. We must acknowledge this, as sometimes our biases get in the way of accepting different ideologies or concepts. Nevertheless, self-worth and its theory are necessary for understanding how our perceptions of ourselves are needed to pinpoint the possible level of our self-esteem, as often, our low self-worth and abasement is a glaring neon sign that our esteem may also be following along this destructive path of self-hatred. But we've focused mainly on how 'self' prompts the formation of self-worth and our self-esteem. What about social expectations, and where do they fall in?

What happens when others' expectations—or even your own—become too much to bear? It spells one word: *catastrophe*.

Heavy Is the Expectation

I hope I'm correct to presume that all of you have had the experience and the heavy weight of expectations placed on you. The pressure from your family, your friends, school, your religious beliefs—if that applies to you—and even the social constructs placed on us are enough to break the proverbial camel's back or the often fragile mentality of our conscious minds. Societal expectations have especially become increasingly weighty in the grand scheme of life. These expectations have become the backbone of how we behave and react to the circumstances surrounding us, with deviances seen as abnormal, weird, or outright incorrect. Societal expectations exist within every stratum or society as each individual is expected to behave in a manner befitting their lot in life.

In addition, there are specific expectations centered around a person's gender, age, and cultural background. Unfortunately, these expectations can often be unrealistic and force people to chase after a mirage in the distance. When the reality that these expectations can never come to fruition, or when the weight of the expectations becomes too excessive to bear, we lose sight of ourselves in the process and may be shunned due to failing to meet these expectations placed before us. Our mentality collapses, making our sense of self-worth and self-esteem crash and sending us into a spiral of unwanted thoughts, behavioral patterns, and adverse emotions targeted at ourselves.

That is not to say societal expectations are inherently wrong; instead, it is always advisable to have a particular goal in mind that we want to achieve. As long as the expectations placed on us are specific, measurable, achievable, relevant, and time-bound, they can be an excellent measuring tool for self-evaluation and assessment, allowing us the opportunity for introspection and reassessment of our goals as per the current situation. The overbearing problem begins when these expectations take a toll on our physical and mental health. For people in the 21st century, surrounded by more unrealistic standards and expectations, the invisible pressure becomes so tangible that it becomes harder to breathe in the maelstrom around us. Before I delve any deeper into how societal expectations promote and encourage the growth of low self-esteem, let's look at what societal expectations are.

Study.com defines societal expectations as the "implicit rules that govern one's reactions and beliefs in a way that is deemed acceptable by society" (Kamberaj, 2022). Kamberaj elaborated on this by stating that societal expectations extend further than the individual; they depend on the individual's cultural retentions, religious beliefs, or ages, with the latter's range, they explained, being more versatile than we would previously believe. Societal expectations differ even in the complexity surrounding the concept of gender, as each gender has different expectations placed on them due to the norms, dictated rules, and pre-existing assigned roles. Such a statement does not mean that societal expectations are static and never-changing. More realistically, our expectations evolve or can remain stagnant as others see fit.

For example, as Katherine C. Powells points out in the article, "The Role of Concept of Self and Societal Expectations in Academic and Career Achievement," the societal expectations of women, in particular, have undergone steady changes, with women no longer limited to the label and expectation of being 'caring,' 'feminine,' or "more emotionally driven" than their male counterparts in the working place (Powells, 2009). That is not to say, however, that these expectations have disappeared into thin air. Nevertheless, there are still glimpses of expectations becoming less societal and more individualistic as time dances onward to its beats.

The article, "The Effects of 'Social Expectation' on the Development of Civil Society in Japan," refers to societal expectations as "internalized social norm[s] for individuals and organizations, thus for society as a whole, about what people should do" (Hasegawa et al., 2007). They expressed that societal expectation is a culmination of public opinion and social agreement in a sphere that, as mentioned by Hasegawa et al., is a given for functioning in life and society (p. 180). Thus expectations have existed since our conception, and we are raised to follow these expectations steadfastly. Any deviance is met with discontent, regardless of the reason for not following societal expectations, even if the individual cannot fulfill these expectations.

As stated earlier, societal expectations differ depending on various factors, but quite potentially, the largest shareholder is the gender factor, with this particular factor promoting the issues that can develop from unrealistic societal expectations. A report by the Pew Research Center puts this ideology to the test. In a survey, "On Gender Differences, No Consensus on Nature vs.

Nurture," the characteristics that are of great value among men and women vary broadly and give uncomfortable statistics of how these societal expectations vary between the genders and raises a few questions as to how the societal gaze has various implications for its citizens (Pew Research Center, 2017). The trait most valued by society from men, according to the respondents, comes at a whopping 33%: honesty or morality. Alternatively, 35% of respondents believed that society places the most significant emphasis on women's physical attractiveness more than any other trait.

In males, physical attractiveness only accounts for 11% of the total respondents—take that as you will. Another more extensive comparison comes from professional or financial success. According to respondents and survey percentage ranges, there is a 15% gap between men and women in that respect (23%, 8%, respectively). Overall, the predominant traits society expects from men are honesty, financial prowess, and strength. Intelligence, family orientation, and politeness are the lowest desirable traits in males, the survey alleged, with all three being below the double-digit percentage mark. Yet, the differences are almost entirely subverted in women. Only 6% of respondents believe that women need to be strong, with the favorable traits skewing to what is commonly denoted as the "traditional woman." The three most desirable qualities in women, as described in the survey, are physical attractiveness, empathy (or the nurturing trait), and intelligence.

So, what does this mean for societal expectations? It is easy to draw lines from this survey. The quickest judgment is that the male and female expectations are far from each other, creating a sense of discordance in their conclusion. While both of the highest percentile traits are overall linked to physiology, this implication appears: Men have, since the dawn of consciousness in humankind, received the label of 'liars' or 'untrustworthy,' and so society demands that a man be honest, or have a high moral standard. However, standards of morality are tinged with many shades of gray, and it is difficult to ascertain the correct measure of character to subscribe to. Alternatively, physical attractiveness is the most desirable trait for women and raises the implication that the most that women have to offer is their beauty, which sets up the harsh reality of beauty worship and idolization. It may even increase the ideology that women are only valuable the more beautiful they are and be heard or not seen. Both implications negatively influence our self-esteem, potentially plummeting said esteem to the lowest point.

For men, the traditional aspects of masculinity are the hallmarks of what is socially acceptable: the financial ability to maintain and care for their family, the strength or toughness needed for a difficult decision, and above all, the added and highly ranked friendliness trait. Physical appearance is mid-tier at best, and intelligence is seen as almost optional in the respondents' understanding of society. Yet, there exists a conundrum: A man is expected to be honest with himself and others—emotionally and physically—but is also pushed to be the head hombre, the macho man. Unfortunately, the idea of strength and masculinity in men has signified that a man who is honest with his thoughts and emotions is weak, and it is better to bottle up this frustration inside and cover it up with a toxic form of masculinity. Pieces of evidence of these are easily found on YouTube, especially among the ranking of 'Alpha' males ranking and the "red-pill, blue-pill, black-pill" male stratosphere.

All of these mentalities perpetuate the toxic masculinity expectation that a man must always not show any emotions, essentially being an emotionless rock in the depths of the sea with no gaps in their strength and always be the conquerors in the assumed battle-royale of relationships. However, such an expectation among adolescent teenage boys spells more harm than benefit. Men fear being seen as weak or the so-called "beta male" or as a 'simp.' In a world where no one wants to conform but still feels the need to fit in, the fear of not meeting these taxing expectations often means these young, impressionable boys lash out their frustrations on others, thus constantly pushing the narrative of men being "visual creatures." That sort of mentality that devalues humans into stereotypical boxes of animalistic nature offers no benefit to others. Instead, it perpetuates a culture and society of insecure men with low self-esteem caused by them failing to measure up to the unrealistic expectations forced upon them.

In women, societal expectations run primarily in the realms of physical attractiveness, and unfortunately, many men and women see women's beauty as their only redeeming quality, along with the expected submissiveness and docility that come with the concept of femininity. A publication by the National Organization for Women offers these statistics for a better understanding of women and the idolization of body image and its insecurities:

- One study reports that at age 13, 53% of American girls are "unhappy with their bodies." This grows to 78% by the time these girls reach 17.

- Half (50%) of teens are 'self-conscious' about their bodies; 26.2% report being 'dissatisfied.'

- By age 60, 28.7% of women feel 'dissatisfied' and 32.6% feel 'self-conscious' about their bodies.

- Many teens (45.5%) report that they are considering cosmetic surgery, and 43.7% of women over 60 report considering this surgery

- Two of elementary school girls' main concerns are about their weight (40%) or about becoming "too fat" (65%).

- A majority of girls (59%) reported dissatisfaction with their body shape, and 66% expressed the desire to lose weight.

- Studies at Stanford University and the University of Massachusetts found that 70% of college women say they feel worse about their own looks after reading women's magazines (National Organization for Women, 2019).

With such a notion rooted in the very framework of our society, it is difficult for women to accept their body image and self-concept as they are. Unrealistic beauty standards, perpetuated since possibly the beginning of time, have forced women to chase after a body that is outside of their reach, prompting them to believe that due to not fitting into this narrative of a particular appeal, they are less than other women who fit the description.

As a result, the cosmetics industry has profited off these women's insecurities, who may believe that happiness derives from our appearances or being what others constitute as the traditional beauty standard of light-colored hair, blue eyes, pale skin, and a thin figure. Or it can be the more buxom imagery derived from African Americans and Africans with wider hips, more significant busts, and thicker lips. With these contrasting images colliding, it is difficult for women in contemporary society to ascertain what standard to fit into. Their insecurities can lead them to multiple medical conditions and maladaptive behaviors, and there is an increased risk of developing an eating disorder due to the warped belief that their body is not thin enough and needs to be slimmed down further. Additionally, such societal expectations increase the risk of depression in women who battle with body image, or body dysmorphia, due to their low self-esteem plummeting in the face of an unrealistic beauty standard they cannot reach in this lifetime.

Yet, societal expectations extend much further than the labels of masculinity and femininity. Quite possibly, you can list a few societal expectations placed on you. However, it is normal for us not to meet these expectations and for you to move along to your unique rhythm and not the beat dictated and indoctrinated in us at a young age. Let's break down a few, shall we?

1. Popularity is a necessity. Not having friends (or a small group) is a no-go. Most people have the now completely used-out phrase "humans are social beings" to be a mantra of sorts to promote the ideology that having more friends equals more popularity, which lends itself to the belief that more popularity means higher levels of happiness. Yet, the concept that humans are social beings does not tell us that we absolutely must subscribe to the narrative that having multiple friendships are the hallmark of a better social life. Some people work and thrive better in smaller groups, which is perfectly fine. Your level of popularity does not define your existence, and being in the background does not diminish who you are. The world is a glorious stage, but this stage would never exist without those hiding behind the folds of the curtain. There is no guarantee for happiness through the idealizing of popularity. After all, all that glitters is not gold, and behind the facade of popularity lies hidden insecurities that many fail to see.

2. Society expects you to excel with at least one activity. I'm not sure where this came about to be honest. Yet, we grow with the expectations to be excellent at something; mediocrity and being average are viewed contemptuously. However, you inevitably will not

excel or be exceptional at something in your fleeting life. And honestly? That, too, is okay. I am not negating that we can't seek a passion or skill to practice and perfect as that would be hypocritical of me. Instead, I am saying that even if you are not the best in your craft, you should never demean or debase yourself due to not excelling at your chosen path. Instead, learn to celebrate the small increments and improvements. Take a step back to look at your work, and be proud to say, "Yes. I did that." Above all, the most crucial aspect is having fun while working. It should be enjoyable, not draining and exhaustive to complete.

3. Follow one linear pathway to adulthood. If there is one thing that is everyday speech heard by everyone at some point in their life is the never-ending (near) droning that we must attend high school, graduate from college, gain a successful job, get married, and have kids. The truth is that not everyone will follow this linear path set out for them. Once again, this is okay. Maybe you want to travel the world or find a different avenue. It is your life, and *you* are the one who decides the path you'll follow. Unfortunately, society perpetuates this feeling of guilt when we indicate that we wish to pursue a wholly differing route and even represses the deviation of what some consider the 'norm.'

Within societal expectations lies 'conformity,' or acting according to predetermined rules and norms. When we cannot conform or subscribe to a particular mentality, we are instantly judged and labeled as something that may not necessarily be the best reflection of ourselves. "Verbatim" by Mother Mother puts this idea into perspective. The singer questions the validity of how a straight person receives such a label. Is it the boxer brief, or is the 12-pound steak? he asks the listeners almost sarcastically. He negates this in the previous line, in which he states that, despite acting in a way commonly linked to femininity or queerness, he is sexually attracted to females. Often, society forces us to conform to its expectations, even at the risk of losing our sense of identity or developing low self-esteem resulting from failing to meet said expectations.

Below, you can view a small checklist for regulating expectations through questioning our intentions (Nelson, n.d.).

- How did I develop this (or these) expectation(s)?

- What is the root cause for these expectations?

- Are they based on my own, or are they merely a reflection of someone else's?

- Will these expectations benefit or hinder me at the stage I am in life?

- What purpose does it serve?

- Am I being fair? Am I evaluating myself justly?

But where does social media fall into all this? Patience, dear Padawan. All will be revealed in due order. Such an order being now.

Click, Edit, Post: The Age of Social Media and Esteem

In contemporary society, a heavy emphasis rests on the concept of "the fast life" and instant gratification. Everything becomes accessible at the tap of the screen or a slide of the thumb. It becomes increasingly easy for us to see and interact with others. The internet is an excellent tool that promotes social interactions through bridging this distance and the ease of accessibility. But what happens due to this ease of access? During this digital revolution, we are now engaging with persons we would never have under different circumstances. Due to this exposure to high dosages, we are now faced with an increased level of persons suffering from low self-esteem and incidences of anxiety and depression. We do this as we compare ourselves to the glamorous lives those on social media seem to portray. And if there is anything we've learned, comparing ourselves to others is more harmful than beneficial, leaving us feeling as though our appearances are not enough. Social media, or rather the people manipulating the various media, have managed to maintain a stranglehold on values, norms, expected behavior, and the appearance of the general public.

How deeply has social media managed to work its way to the point that our entire sense of self-esteem hinges on the validation and acceptance of others to exist? To answer this question, we must first glance at the concept of social comparison.

APA Dictionary describes social comparison as "the proposition that people evaluate their abilities and attitudes concerning those of others in a process that plays a significant role in self-image and subjective well-being" (APA Dictionary of Psychology, 2022g). Alternatively, others define it as the phenomenon that occurs when we compare ourselves with others, particularly our abilities and characteristics (Bergagna & Tartaglia, 2018). Bergagna and Tartaglia continue this reasoning by suggesting that this predisposition may be a personality trait that lends itself to the tendency to compare others with ourselves. That is, persons with a certain degree 0f uncertainty and instability in line with their perceived level of self-worth or those more sensitively motivated to the nuances of others tend to the archetype that compares themselves with others.

APA Dictionary explains that "social comparison" is not limited to only comparing oneself with others perceived to be better than ourselves (or 'upward' social comparison). We also compare ourselves with those we deem less than ourselves ('downward' social comparison) or make comparisons with those who are, in our judgment, in a similar position as ourselves ('lateral' social comparison) (APA Dictionary of Psychology, 2022g). Additionally, social comparisons are more rooted in cultures that value the idea of a consensus or one solid narrative everyone follows, as stated by Baldwin and Mussweiler (2018). As such, social comparisons become rife in a culture or society promoting the narrative of collectivism or where the fitting of a pre-described mold is encouraged as the correct perspective.

Social media ties into social comparison as its foundations are built around the concept of collectivism or a sense of united thinking in its various niches and subsections. There is a niche for nearly every radical or potentially damaging subculture. Social media is the gateway drug for many belief systems, from the incel community to the localized mess that is the R/Reddit posts. When we have a particular narrative or are inclined to head to one, social media feeds into these ideologies with neat little niches tailor-made for each perspective.

I will not be the one to trod down upon social media as the very roots and intentions of social media are, in fact, relatively neutral. It is nothing more than a method of connecting with those you know and other strangers and can be a place of comfort and safety for prominent persons despite their 'real-life' situations and circumstances. Even more remarkable, it is a source of finance for many people and can be an effective tool for positive social interactions. However, it also allows for a breeding ground of insecurities and low self-esteem. As the world becomes more digitized and information and videos become increasingly easier to access, more people stare at their social media accounts, with maybe the most commonly repeated thought in this generation: "Am I pretty or cool enough? Like all these other people? Am I good enough?" Unfortunately, the answer we make to these spiral thoughts is often a resounding 'No.'

The idea of the heading "Click, Edit, Post" should be able to summarize the reality of what social media has now become. Most, if not everything, of what we see are what I would affectionately label as "Curated for Views." We all see the gorgeous women and men with the seemingly unattainable golden ratio, see them going on multiple vacations, luxury tours, driving expensive cars, in essence, living the best life imaginable. Often, we may look at these persons and almost instinctively think, *Oh my God, I wish I could live like this. What am I doing with myself?* Do not lie; I know that little intrusive thought has popped up more times than you can count. We compare ourselves to them and imagine what we could do in their place. I do not believe initiating a comparison is an inherently harmful thing to do. Comparisons can aid us in taking a step back, reconfiguring and reassessing our current goal in life, and using bits of these comparisons to highlight some missing details can be highly beneficial. However, social media, comparisons, and self-esteem become ugly when we place too much emphasis on what we see on social media, compare and judge ourselves too harshly, and force ourselves to overcompensate for these perceived lackings we have.

In the article, "Increases in Depressive Symptoms, Suicide-Related Outcomes, and Suicide Rates Among U.S. Adolescents After 2010 and Links to Increased New Media Screen Time," Twenge et al. (2017) state that in two surveys based in the United States of America and with an age range of 8–13 of over 500,000 respondents, there has been a marked increase in the appearance of depressive symptoms, attempted suicide and suicide rates in adolescents, more notably among females. They said adolescents who spend more time on social media are more likely to report having mental health issues than their peers who engage more in what is classified as "real-life" or offscreen activities, such as sports.

Another over-arching effect is the concept of over-stimulation of beauty. In the world of beauty, filters, and influencers, there has been a marked decrease in positive identification of body image. The phrase "over-stimulation of beauty" has made its rounds on TikTok, popularized by a user, Elanor Stern. In a video, Stern (2022) speaks of the article "Instagram Face" by Jia Tolentino, in which she states that in a world where beauty has become narrowed down to one particular preference, or what they referred to as 'cyborgian,' which gives major dystopian vibes, as one user comments. In essence, it prompts the perspective of how social media has promoted a singular facial construct to be the hallmark of beauty. As Stern and Tolentino put it, it's a noticeably Caucasian face, with just enough ethnic ambiguity to not let persons label it as 'appropriation' or try to push down the popularity of the facial structure. It can give the illusion that everyone can look this way and prompts unrealistic expectations that all women can and must look like this. If they do not or skew to non-conventional features, women are labeled as the grossly overused and honestly useless term of 'mid' in a bid to describe the supposed averageness of their features.

Along with this face, the idea of a woman having a slender waist, large breasts, wide hips, and a plump rear end has become even more propagated among social media users. While it is not a new fad, it has become alarmingly prevalent, especially as body augmentations have become more accessible, and women are pressured more to fit a constrictive mold. Some women chase this fantasy of perfect features and are uncomfortable in their skin. Others can become depressed and develop different mental illnesses and eating disorders in response to these taxing expectations.

However, men also fall victim to this overexposure of opinions, despite more research on the 'fairer' gender. In contemporary society, many offensive labels are thrown around if men do not fit a particular image of what they are allegedly supposed to emulate physically and mentally. There are expectations of having a specific body type, regardless of the how's and why's. If they do not, they receive belittlement from other males and sometimes females. The concept of this body type focuses not on keeping healthy or maintaining a particular lifestyle; it subsists on insisting that a man must have this specific form, and anything opposite to it is weak or attractive. Gültzow et al. (2020) elaborate on this in their journal article, "Male Body Image Portrayals on Instagram."

> Nowadays, men are faced with sociocultural influences giving rise to the desire for a muscular and lean body, resulting in men facing body dissatisfaction, which is associated with health consequences such as depression and eating pathology. One of the sociocultural influences playing a role in the development of body dissatisfaction is ideal body type portrayal on media platforms. Men face a standard emphasizing muscularity and leanness in both traditional and social media. (Gültzow et al., 2020)

In addition, social media helps to perpetuate the toxic masculinity trend of men bottling up their emotions as showing emotions is seen as an inherently feminine action, unbecoming of a "true man." Jasiah Arrington on TikTok offers a few examples of toxic masculinity. Delivered in a dry tone, Arrington says that toxic masculinity includes assigning colors to a specific gender, the need to state that they are not gay, and stating that males do not cry because that is not what men do (Arrington, 2021). Unfortunately, the impressionable generation within contemporary society quickly latches on to these ideologies and feel pressured to act in a way that they believe is correct or manly. They become afraid of turning into terms used as a form of insult (beta male, simp), as they seek approval and validation of the men they see on the social media pages. These impressionable boys—and at times, grown men—believe that this is the only acceptable way of acting for a man and think less of themselves if they do not—or can't—meet the standards of the men pushing these toxic mindsets.

Unfortunately, this can result in the constant cycle of impressionable young men having grossly inaccurate thoughts of what being a man constitutes and then spreading these thoughts to other impressionable males. Such a scenario gives rise to incidences of increased aggression and violent tendencies, none of which bodes well for any aspect of the spectrum. According to Schlichthorst et al. (2019), "male suicide is often linked to men's reluctance to seek help for emotional problems, which in turn is influenced by certain dominant masculine norms like self-reliance, invulnerability, and avoidance of expressing emotions."

In essence, the perpetuation of toxic masculinity causes an uptick in the rates of poor mental health issues in males, especially with the ideology that "men do not think with their hearts or emotions, but with their heads." Rage is an actual emotion, but it often seems to be negated. Sadness, guilt, regret, and any other emotions that would mean a man might need to seek help are so often pushed aside in lieu of keeping up that masculine appearance.

As previously stated, social media is not a leviathan, spreading its vile tentacles to wrap up the unsuspecting masses into warped and detrimental thinking. However, persons have been able to extend their beliefs, thought processes, and an idealized version of themselves, which only serves to hurt others in the process. But what does this mean for our health, both physically and mentally?

A whole lot.

Chapter 4: Health and Low Self-Esteem

"And I'm staring into the void again; no one knows what a mess I'm in. The voices in my head say, 'I'm just being paranoid.' But it is bad for my health, how much I hate myself. I suffocate; the weight, it pulls me underneath. Put me out of my misery. My mind feels like an archenemy; can't look me in the eyes. I don't know what hurts the most, holding on or letting go. Reliving my memories, and they're killing me one by one."—"1x1," by Bring Me The Horizon and Nova Twins

While the lead singer of the band, Oliver Sykes, mentions that the primary intention of the song was to address the guilt we carry due to our hateful acts, the piece can also be read as a cry for help from the negative and detrimental thoughts (Bring Me The Horizon and Nova Twins, 2020).

Low Self-Esteem and Physiology

While low self-esteem is often associated more with mental health, it also has detrimental effects on the physiology of humans as a result. Someone can easily start to develop unhealthy habits that can, in turn, lead to worsening damage to the physiology of the person. The thoughts that we have—overall and about ourselves personally—are what help us to create our actions.

One of these unhealthy habits is a negative outlook on your physical appearance. If someone falls into the line of thinking that they hate their body and lets themselves get dragged down into the mired spiral, it can be hazardous to one's physical well-being. People often try starting out on a diet and exercise routine, which is one of many ways to help your mind and body feel much better. However, if they do not quickly start to see the kind of results they were looking for, the healthy diet they were on could easily turn into an eating disorder, putting their body into starvation mode. The fun workout sessions could shift to excessive workouts that are too intense or last for hours, leaving you to feel exhausted in every sense of the word.

The excessive use of drugs or alcohol is also a huge risk when handling low self-esteem. It is all too easy to forget that pain, escape from your reality for a few hours, and then become reliant on them to function. It is dangerous in general to use drugs or alcohol more than recommended by your doctor. However, when the use becomes excessive and you find yourself needing that escape whenever your thoughts about yourself turn dark, that's when you really need to be careful. It is at this point that people often start to use far too much, sometimes leading to fatal alcohol poisoning or overdose.

Finding yourself in a situation where these unhealthy habits have become a part of your life is not easy. There are other ways to help you learn self-confidence and give you the boost that you need! It's time to figure out other ways to boost your confidence that do not make you feel like the nub of a burned-out candle. It would also be a good idea to make an appointment with your doctor if you can do so. Seeking help does not make you weak. Instead, it shows that you are strong enough to make the hard decisions.

Aside from the more obvious associated issues listed above, spiral thoughts of not being good enough can lead you to feel constantly tired, and even physically weak. *It's not worth it to get out of bed. I don't deserve to have a good cup of coffee. I'll just stay home.* Sound familiar? A lot of us who have dealt with low self-esteem are all too familiar with that line of thinking. What this does is cause us to stay home, not get any fresh air or have some fun, and we end up moving less and sitting more.

When these dark thoughts try to stick around and become dark manifestations in your life, preventing you from living your best life. Don't listen! Ignore them! I know that's much easier said than done. Try to distract your mind and body until the thoughts leave you alone; Take a long walk or even just go on a quick, scenic drive. Keep yourself active in mind, body, and spirit.

Many people are not just affected physically. Your mind starts to become indifferent. This very frequently goes hand-in-hand with developing both depression and anxiety. The constant, nagging thought of being inferior to others, of not being good enough, can often make you give up and not want to do the things that you used to love. Relationships suffer, your hobbies go out the window, and even your work suffers while you spiral further.

Have you been noticing that your favorite hobbies and usual pastimes are not giving you what they used to? Or that these activities that you used to love, you no longer enjoy? If so, then ask yourself why. If your reasoning has something to do with what others think or say, do not entertain those thoughts. Your hobbies are for you, not for anyone else's judgment. If they don't like it, they can find their own hobbies and work on themselves. While it can be hard to just stop worrying about what others think, you deserve to get rid of the negativity and toxicity in your own mind, at the very least. Allow yourself to have a little fun! Everyone deserves that! We all need some inspiration and creativity to make this life a little more worth living sometimes!

A more emotional aspect of constantly dealing with low self-esteem is that you often end up angry at yourself, which means you are likely to take out that anger on others. Not looking the way you feel that you are supposed to, or not being able to control your thoughts more, can be very frustrating to deal with. The low self-esteem that causes this frustration also causes you to be disappointed in yourself, and oftentimes angry.

When we take the anger that we have for ourselves out on others, they don't understand that the anger doesn't truly have anything to do with them. This can cause problems with coworkers, managers, family, friends, and partners. They do not deserve your anger, and neither do you.

The frequent anger and stress that low self-esteem can cause often leads to heart disease as well as problems with your blood pressure. This can cause damage to your blood vessels, and then your heart and even kidneys. If the low self-esteem that you are dealing with is causing anger problems, please see a doctor and explain the situation. It is best if they can help you learn to manage all of these feelings for your overall well-being.

It's never easy to pull yourself from that murky spiral of low self-esteem. However, we are all beautiful inside and out. You are good enough. You are deserving. You deserve forgiveness from yourself. Keep reminding yourself of these things daily and learn how to feel better and learn how to start loving yourself.

Another aspect of what low self-esteem can influence is seen in our body language, the way that our subconscious mind presents us. Slouching is already known to cause a multitude of problems from chronic fatigue and weak muscles to osteoarthritis in areas of the neck and spine.

Fatigue itself is also a commonly seen side effect of dealing with bad self-esteem. A lot of your energy is going towards internalizing all of those negative feelings of guilt, anger, sadness, etc. and not enough energy is left to deal with the rest of your needs. Intense emotions drain your emotional energy. Energy is finite and has its limits. Everyone has a certain amount of energy that they can spend on processing and understanding hard and overwhelming emotions. If all of your energy is spent on this, you don't have nearly as much energy for your other tasks, wants, and needs.

Body dysmorphic disorder is another common problem that plagues people that handle low self-esteem. This is a disorder that actually makes it worse most of the time. It causes you to constantly think about and see the flaws or defects in your personality or appearance. This can sometimes lead to self-harming behavior or even suicide. Studies have also shown a high-risk link between low self-esteem and certain eating disorders. Eating disorders are classified as psychiatric disorders because they don't just make one eat too much or too little. They can cause the body to starve itself to death because of someone's dietary restrictions that they placed upon themselves, or even overexertion (Exercising too intensely or for too long, such as mentioned above).

Some studies show how easily having low self-esteem can lead to developing expensive and unhealthy habits such as drinking or smoking. Substance abuse is another possibility after dealing with low self-esteem for a long time. However, there are a lot of other factors that go into someone developing an addiction. Genetics, relationships, support system, and a dozen other factors play into that. It is important, however, to note that many people end up on the bad side of drugs because they have been dealing with low self-esteem by themselves for far too long.

Mental Health and Low Self-Esteem

There is a lot of overlap in the mental health community between low self-esteem, depression, anxiety, and suicidal ideations. According to many of the studies that have so far been done, self-esteem can be a strong indicator of depression, extreme anxiety, or a comorbid diagnosis of both anxiety and depression. Both of these can ultimately lead to an unpleasant end.

As of right now, not many mental health professionals are understanding that seeing low self-esteem in a person is a good time to get a treatment plan discussed. Low self-esteem may be a stand-alone issue, but, more often than not, it can lead to worsening mental and physical health problems in the future. Better to nip it in the bud before it gets more extreme or more detrimental to the individual!

If you or someone close to you has been noticing that your self-esteem is taking a dive, it would be best to talk with your doctor and see what the best course of action is. There are options for you to get help before things get too dark for you and you end up in that unending spiral that has led to so much loss.

Currently, many studies are indicating that it would be wise to treat low self-esteem as a potential precursor to depression, anxiety, and suicidal ideations. While having low self-esteem might not lead to worsening mental health, it can still be treated with the help of a professional! Healthcare professionals in most fields that work directly with patience should start taking note of things such as this. It could very well save lives.

Depression

The risk of developing depression by the time a person is out of adolescence has a lot to do with the self-esteem that has grown within them. If you look at someone who has grown up poorly, seeing all manner of gorgeous and unattainable appearances throughout television and social media but never being able to see the beauty in themselves, you will be looking at someone with low self-esteem. One of the many effects that low self-esteem can have on the mind is causing depression or worsening depression, if one is already prone to it. Depression, even by itself, is very detrimental in many ways. Coupled with or caused by low self-esteem, it can lead to far worse, including suicidal ideation.

People with depression often have a hard time taking care of themselves. Self-care and the love of your hobbies go out the window and motivation to get work done feels non-existent. The idea that someone who is depressed has a hard time getting out of bed in the morning is truer than some people make it seem! Getting up out of bed can feel like a painstakingly difficult chore. Some eat almost nothing when depressed, while others binge eat. Both ways of coping with food are bad for the body and can actually make depression even worse.

Most of the time, people with depression do not look depressed. We are seen putting on a brave front. Being seen as weak, pathetic, or "less than" does not have much appeal when your self-esteem is already at a low point in your life. Please do not make the mistake of seeing someone smile and assuming that they do not deal with depression just like you do.

There are a few ways to cope and get by while dealing with depression. First and foremost, get help! Yes, it is okay to not be okay. However, do you really want to not be okay? Getting help from a professional does not make you weak. It makes you strong enough to survive. Too many people each year deal with depression until it becomes too much for them. Handling mental health problems is never easy, and it never will be. However, it can be done.

In the meantime, here are a few little ways to help yourself cope until you are ready to get the help you may need:

- Journaling. Sometimes writing down what is causing us to feel the way that we do can help tremendously. Throughout history, people have learned that keeping a private journal helps them to keep track of their thoughts, feelings, triggers, and the wondrous number of good things that happen throughout the day, even when they do not realize these good things right away. Try something for me. Each night before bed, I want you to write down five good things that happened during the day. It does not have to be big! It can be as simple as the coffee tasting perfect or the sun shining. These good things can be as extravagant as getting a promotion at work, or as basic as your favorite show finally being added to your favorite streaming service! Try to pinpoint at least five different good things during your day and write them down.

● Self-care. When taking care of yourself seems like an impossible task, there are a few ways to combat it. If you can't bring yourself to brush your teeth, just swish with some mouthwash. It isn't perfect, but no one is. It is a temporary fix. If you can't get up the energy to take even a quick shower, then grab a washcloth, wet and soap it, and wash yourself up with it.

● Exercise. Doing some exercise can have great effects on dealing with depression. When we exercise, our brains release endorphins and we get the rush of 'feel-good' emotions. When we are depressed, it's not always easy to exercise. Try to find just five minutes during your day, even if it's not planned and just a random five minutes that you can handle. Walk, jog, even hula-hoop in place. Do a few minutes of just stretching! You've got this.

Anxiety

Anxiety is depression's neurotic cousin. We all know someone with anxiety or deal with it in our own life, and while it certainly comes with its own set of callous rules, it often coexists in our brains with its cousin, depression.

Anxiety and the symptoms that come with it often can stem from or cause low self-esteem. Anxiety can destroy your confidence and make you feel so much worse about yourself, causing your self-esteem to sink even further. When your inner voice is constantly saying things such as *this outfit looks horrible on me, they're staring!* or *things are never going to work out, I'm just not worth it*, then it's hard not to listen. Sound familiar? Having low self-esteem sets you up to have a lot of anxiety in the future. If you have anxiety already, then it can cause worsening self-esteem. It is a vicious cycle in which it can be difficult to drag yourself out.

It does not have to end there, though it often feels like it will. There is a lot of help out there for people who suffer from anxiety and low self-esteem. Speaking to your doctor about it can be a great way to get help. If you don't want medication, and many people don't for various reasons, there are still many more tools that a doctor can recommend, such as several forms of therapy.

Anxiety attacks are no joke and can be downright terrifying to deal with on a regular basis. It can often feel like you are having a heart attack, or you might have a feeling of impending doom. If you find yourself in the midst of an anxiety attack and you are not sure what to do, here is a helpful tip:

- Close your eyes and take a couple of deep breaths.

- When you open your eyes, identify five blue objects (the sky, a flower, anything blue).

- Next, identify four green objects (grass, a drink, etc.).

- Third, identify three yellow objects (the sun, paper, etc.).

- Fourth, identify two red objects (a flower, clothing, etc.).

● Finally, look around and identify one purple object near you.

This tip has helped many people when trying to come down from having an anxiety or panic attack. Focusing on specific things like colors can help your mind feel more ordered and less chaotic, leading you to make more rational decisions and think clearly again.

Suicide

This is not an easy subject to navigate, for any of us. This topic is one of the reasons why the trigger warning at the beginning of this book was included. Not everyone is willing to speak about this, and even fewer people are able or willing to get the proper help that they need. There are a lot of resources for those who feel that things have reached a hopeless point and feel that there is no coming back for them. Some of these resources will be posted later in the book in case you need access to them.

There have been several studies that show the link between lower self-esteem and a higher rate of suicide or suicidal ideation. When you feel like you are not worth the time, effort, and energy of others or that you are a burden, suicide can seem like a simple, tidy, quick ending to a long life of frustration, disappointment, and pain. People do not always see that there is still hope left or realize the pain they are leaving behind for the people that knew and loved them.

Reasons abound in life revolving around why someone might develop lower self-esteem than others: traumatic or neglectful childhood, school problems in adolescence, money problems from childhood on up, chronic illnesses, or other physical problems that cause dysphoria and dysmorphia, whether real or perceived. Regardless of why we have ended up the way that we have, it is not too late to drag ourselves out of this pit.

Chapter 5: Miscellaneous Thoughts on Low Self-Esteem

"I understand, I'm a liability, get you wild, make you leave, I'm a little much for everyone"—"Liability" by Lorde

While low self-esteem can have many starting points, money trouble is one of the biggest culprits and more common causes. It's never easy to admit that you are having financial difficulties—plenty of people have waited until it was far too late to tell anyone—but it is crucial, for the benefit of your mental and physical health, to take care of things while there is a chance to fix it.

More often than we realize, people are willing to listen and help if they can. Whether it is a family member, a friend, a trusted coworker, a therapist, or simply your own journal...talk about the issue. Take things one day at a time and one step at a time. Nothing is solved in just one day. Making small changes over the course of weeks or months can have long-lasting effects.

Money Worries

The stresses that can occur with money, or the lack thereof, can actually prompt the development of low self-esteem among the populace. People who do not make enough money to cover bills or who are just scraping by have a lot of financial stress. In addition, throughout most cultures, there is a common theme that people with more money get more respect and seem to live happier lives. Seeing yourself not deserving more respect can crush your self-esteem because you have learned that in most of society that the ones with the money, the power, and respect, deserve it all.

On the other hand, however, you could actually sabotage your own success and wealth because of low self-esteem. *I'll never get this done by the deadline, or I'm never going to get the promotion, my coworker is a much better choice*, probably feel like common thoughts that rattle around in your mind. Once you get stuck in that mental spiral, self-sabotage becomes a very real issue.

Your self-esteem and work/life experiences feed from and influence each other. If you emanate low self-esteem, then your work suffers and you are less likely to have the success that you are looking for. On the reverse side, the more your work suffers, all of those times you were passed over for that promotion, or other work/life difficulties, can cause your self-esteem to take a serious dive.

There is good news in this regard! Studies (Nauert, 2015) have shown that people with more money, more success, or higher financial-social status, do not change their happiness very much in comparison to someone who works an average job or is making just enough money for bills.

So, I pose this question to you: Does money really buy happiness, or is happiness more a matter of perspective?

The Professional and Self-Esteem

Professionals and persons within the general working population are often victims of developing low self-esteem issues, especially when the social comparison is often much higher among the working populace. People within your working environment are much more likely to make you feel as though success is a contest, and if you do not win, then you are not worthy.

Unfortunately, there is this trope that if you are a professional, you need to exude self-confidence and charisma. Worse still, setting yourself up against such high standards often means a much further fall. Expectations, from ourselves and others alike that are too high can be a serious cause of low self-esteem. It causes us to oppress our true selves and put on this facade of confidence, digging ourselves deeper into that hole.

Bullies and Self-Esteem

Oftentimes, bullies are viewed as persons who have low self-esteem, as they lash out in a bid to cover their own insecurities. While this can be true, it begs the question of how factual this statement is. Recent studies have shown that bullies, the aggressors, have an inflated sense of self-esteem, higher levels of confidence, and even lower levels of depression. In these instances, coupled with the need to feel powerful and superior to others, these higher senses of self can lead some people to be aggressive, destructive, and downright cruel to people they feel are weaker than they are.

On the flip side, victims of bullying, both in childhood and adulthood, tend to develop lower self-esteem than their aggressive counterparts. Does bullying cause low self-esteem, or do people with low self-esteem tend to attract bullies? Both pathways and scenarios are equally likely. Regardless of the why, there are ways of coping with being bullied, and ways to get yourself out of such a bad situation.

Chapter 6: It's Okay to Fail

"Cause I feel like I'm the worst, so I always act like I'm the best"—"Oh no!" by Marina and The Diamonds

Self-esteem and its complications often arise from misplaced conceptions related to self-worth and can stem from feelings of inadequacies and repeated failures. Be careful of falling into the trap of toxic positivity—it is okay to fail. It's how we humans learn! You are no less human, no less amazing, or worth any less because you fail sometimes. It means that you are strong enough to keep trying.

Instead of burying your emotions beneath the surface and keeping that ever-constant smile on your face, understand that it is okay to feel exactly how you feel right now. All too often people seem to think that if we are feeling any negative emotions, then we are bad or doing something wrong. The reality is that 'bad' emotions are just as normal as 'good' ones and are a completely natural part of life. Pretending to be perfectly fine when you need help will only end up with you isolating yourself when you need a support system the most.

It's Okay to Not Feel Okay

The crushing weight of expectations often leaves people feeling antagonistic about themselves, and they are left feeling as though they have no right to feel such emotions. It's okay to not feel the best each and every day. We are only human in the end, but there is also a need to recognize when we are heading in the complete opposite direction of growth and healing.

Pushing aside all of those negative feelings and thoughts, suppressing the bad, will only make them stronger until they are a crushing weight, overwhelming you with negativity. Instead, acknowledge the pain, depression, or anger. Process it, and learn to understand and accept those feelings. It is perfectly okay to feel exactly how you are feeling right at this moment. It's okay to be angry or sad. It's okay to feel broken. Understanding and accepting these bad emotions gives you the room to heal.

When we try to avoid all of these negative emotions, these actions tell our brains that the emotions are bad or dangerous. When our mind says that something is dangerous, our body will respond as it is trained to do. We put ourselves in fight, flight, freeze, or fawn mode, and this can have detrimental effects on both our mind and body. This can also cause a lot of sleep problems, including varying forms of insomnia. It can also cause a rapid heartbeat, stress on the heart that can lead to a worsening condition, shallow or rapid breathing, or even symptoms of post-traumatic stress disorder (PTSD).

Learning From Your Mistakes

An important facet of self-esteem is acknowledging certain topics and uncomfortable truths. Learning from previous mistakes is a healthy measure to undertake, and quite a difficult pill to swallow as a fundamental aspect of growing confidence and understanding yourself in the process. This can aid in improving self-esteem and inspire self-love and confidence.

In the time of our distant ancestors, when making a simple mistake could be incredibly costly, leading to serious injury or even death, humans had to develop ways to change the way they did things to ensure a safe future. When we make a mistake, we often get that sinking feeling in our stomach or we can feel ourselves cringe from it. This is not a bad thing, though it can feel like that. It happens so that our brain has a chance to record the mistake and find another way around it. Our mind tries to minimize the number of times the same mistakes are repeated so that we can grow. However, some of us take a few extra times of making the same mistakes as others, and that's okay too!

The most difficult part of this process is the very first step: accepting full responsibility for your role in making that mistake. You made the decision that caused this. Acknowledge that and tell yourself, *I messed up, but I will do better*. The phrase "to err is human" is absolutely true. We all make mistakes, far more frequently than many of us would like to admit. However, until you are ready to own up to the fact that you have made this error, you will not be ready for the changes that you want to make.

Once you are ready to own up to your mistakes, the next step is to make yourself a plan. It will not do you any good to continue beating yourself up over your mistake. Instead, keep yourself held accountable for the problems and make a plan to focus on doing better and attempting to not repeat the same mistakes. All human error has a valuable lesson within it. Sometimes, it can even help to create a list of reasons to not repeat that same mistake. Put it on a sticky note and post it near your bed!

Working on these things and learning to better yourself through the experiences that your mistakes will bring you can lead to having higher self-discipline. Treat self-discipline as a muscle as the more you work on it, the stronger it will be. With higher self-discipline comes confidence. Having confidence in yourself—not arrogance, that is a whole other beast to tackle—is vital to your well-being, both physically and emotionally. It will boost your self-esteem and help you to make better choices. Overall, developing your confidence is crucial to boosting your self-esteem and thriving in your life the way that you deserve to.

In this next chapter, we will explore just how we can go about building our confidence and self-esteem. While we are working on our self-discipline, there is hope for a better future for those like us.

Chapter 7: Building Confidence and Self-Esteem

"It's bad when you annoy yourself, so irritating, don't wanna be my friend no more, I wanna be somebody else"—"Don't Let Me Get Me" by Pink (2001) Even beautiful and talented celebrities such as Pink battle with low self-esteem at times. During an interview after her album featuring this song debuted, she revealed that she, too, has to fight "a war against the mirror."

Reflecting

Our deepest fear is not that we are inadequate. Our deepest fear is that we are powerful beyond measure. It is our light, not our darkness that most frightens us. We ask ourselves, Who am I to be brilliant, gorgeous, talented, fabulous? Actually, who are you not to be? You are a child of God. Your playing small does not serve the world. There is nothing enlightened about shrinking so that other people won't feel insecure around you. We are all meant to shine, as children do. We were born to manifest the glory of God that is within us. It is not just in some of us; It is in everyone. And as we let our own light shine, we unconsciously permit other people to do the same. As we are liberated from our own fear, our presence automatically liberates others. (Williamson, 1996/2012)

When Marianne Williamson wrote this in her book *A Return to Love: Reflections on the Course of Miracles*, people were abounding with opinions on what she truly meant. People tend to believe that they fear they are not good enough, not adequate, and fear failure. Most people simply accept that this is what stops them from truly growing and developing in this life. They accept that they are inadequate instead of finding the root of the problems.

This quote from her book flips this way of thinking around. It says instead that people may believe that the main reason they aren't living their very best life or making a huge difference somewhere in the world is really just self-deception. The true reason that a person is held back in their life is that they fear just how powerful they truly are. They fear that they really could change the world and are afraid to experience and acknowledge that such power lies within them. Instead, they just hide behind this kind of false fear that they are not good enough. Therefore, they simply do not even try to create such wonder in their life and the world. Your light holds so much more power than you realize.

The Steps to Self-Esteem

It is all too easy to speak negativity into your life, and it is just easy to fall prey to self-destructive thoughts. Building your self-confidence and esteem is a difficult process, but the feelings of self-worth and valuing yourself are well worth the arduous journey to self-discovery. In this chapter, we will be detailing some great steps that you can take to build your self-esteem.

Step One: Negativity, Begone!

The very first step to building self-esteem is to remove the mental roadblocks and dissenting voices that are built on self-deprecating thoughts and beliefs. Many of these mental hurdles are simple concepts, but not always easy to overcome. Fear of change or failure, for example, can cripple our motivation and cause us to give up before we ever truly give something a try. After all, if you don't try, then you can't fail, right? Unfortunately, all this does is prevent us from seeing what we are truly capable of and from realizing our true potential.

Figuring out the mental roadblocks that are preventing you from living your best life starts with developing your self-awareness. Start by writing down your goals. Make a list of what you want out of life, but be sure to leave some space to make notes on each goal. It can be as little as one or two things, or you can fill pages of a journal. Assess your own mind to find what you really want. Some people find that meditation can help with this.

Once you have your list, think about how to get yourself to that point. If you don't know some of them, that's okay! For the rest, make a small plan. Write out the very next steps that you would need to take to set these plans in motion. Is it to start the morning with a healthier breakfast? Is it to apologize to that person you hurt? Getting your goals on a roll and building momentum can help you replace the negativity and mental roadblocks with determination.

If your mind is still spiraling with negative thoughts while you work on your self-awareness, there are some tips you can use to stop them in their tracks. Ask yourself if that thought was an accurate depiction of the situation, or if it was just a negative blip that popped in uninvited. If it is realistic, that's okay! You can fix it. Recognize it and then challenge it. Try to find one good thing that could come from this situation. If your family member or friend had the same thought, what would you tell them?

Step Two: See the Beauty of Your Soul; Exploring the Inner Person

After challenging the negative thought process, it is time to go inwards and see the beauty of the soul, despite all its flaws and jagged edges, and see the positive sides of yourself. It is time to see the good in you. Identifying our good points is a necessary step for establishing our self-worth.

While it is frustratingly easy to get caught up in the spiral of everything that is going wrong, stopping that process and turning it around is vital. Find another page in that journal and write down the things that you are good at. Are you a great cook or baker? Write it down and do that activity more! Are you a great athlete? Write it down and sign up for a marathon! Find the things that you are good at, things that you like to do, and find more activities, or even careers, to develop your skills further.

Try to write down at least three things that you are good at and put that list in a place where you will see it often, such as on your nightstand or even by your mirror.

Steps Three and Four: Removing Toxicity and Finding "Me Time"

Oftentimes, low self-esteem can be attributed to the relationships built, and the people we are surrounded by. Removing toxic and harmful persons from our lives is a huge milestone in promoting self-esteem and building positive and healthy outlooks and relationships. This can be a game-changer in how we perceive and value ourselves, leading to much higher self-esteem.

If you find that spending time with specific people in your life is only bringing your mood down, then try spending less time with those people. You don't have to avoid them altogether, but a break would be a good start. Alternatively, if you feel comfortable talking to them about it, you could try to gently tell them how their words or actions make you feel. Explain to them that you value their friendship and deserve to be treated well.

Expanding on the realization that you deserve a good life, just like everyone else does, learn to say no. If you overburden yourself because you agree to everything people ask of you, all that will happen is you become more stressed out, anxious, depressed, and have a lower sense of self-worth because you can't handle everything you've agreed to! Saying 'no' typically will not destroy your relationships, as it's a normal part of being human. Children are more than happy to tell their adults 'no' when they don't want to do something they were asked to. Adults have that same right.

In addition to helping rid yourself of the toxicity in your life, find some time to breathe. Don't make plans for the weekend. Whatever you need to get done for that weekend, get it done the day before. Over the weekend, spend time getting to know yourself again and doing what you love. If that means vegging on the couch and playing video games, then do it! If it means a long soak in a hot bubble bath and getting a peel-off face mask, relax and enjoy it. Just be you, getting to know you, for the weekend. You might just find that you want to do this more often. Good. You deserve it.

Step Five: Affirm Your Self-Worth and Challenge Yourself

Affirming your self-worth is a daunting task and is often where many fall short. Challenging yourself is one of the most "tried-and-true" methods of affirming your value as a person. In addition to being incredibly helpful on your journey to higher self-esteem, it can also be fun to challenge yourself! We all have times when we feel nervous because we are about to try something new or engage in an unfamiliar challenge, but that is no reason to just avoid it altogether.

Instead, set yourself a goal. Starting small is the easiest way to develop this into a positive habit. Join an exercise class or group, take a class or two, or even just set a goal to drink more water! Achieving your goals, whatever they are, is a great way to develop higher self-esteem. You can do this if you truly want to make these positive changes in your life.

Chapter 8: Positive Affirmations—An Introduction

"Hiding under the bed, in my body, in my head, why won't somebody come and save me from this, make it end?"—"Monster" by Skillet

Affirmations have become a huge staple in the spiritual and healing side of the internet. But what is an affirmation, and is it always a helpful method of promoting optimism and wellness? Many people swear by the use of positive affirmations to make the changes they want in life. On the other hand, there are many skeptics, just as with any type of spirituality.

What Are Affirmations?

In its simplest and purest form, an affirmation is a sentence or phrase that you repeat in your mind, to yourself, or to others.

For any change to happen, actions have to shift. In order to change your actions, you have to start by changing your thoughts. Affirmations have been known to aid in this, helping you to alter your thought patterns. Positive affirmations can bring about great changes in you. People often use some type of affirmation every day without even realizing it. "I'm never going to get this job" is a very familiar one for a lot of people. "I deserve this" is also very common when dealing with a bad situation. These are negative affirmations, but people do not always realize this. Changing these types of thought patterns until it is a habit to use phrases such as "I am strong and capable" or "I can accomplish anything I set my mind to" can be a great tool to utilize in your journey.

These thoughts and phrases are kept short to make sure that they are cemented in our memory. When we have those negative thoughts inevitably pop back up, you can redirect them back into positive ones with the use of affirmations. They help you to become more self-aware and more aware of your own thought patterns. This is incredibly helpful because a lot of our thoughts are subconscious, and this can eventually help to stop negative thoughts before they even start.

Positive affirmations can be used to boost your self-esteem, motivate yourself to make positive changes in your life, and learn to stop the negative cycles. When your thoughts are happier, then all of you is happier, too.

Positive and Negative Affirmations

Just as with every other instance within life, affirmations can be negative as well, despite the general concept of affirmations being defaulted to be positive. For those of us with low self-esteem, it can feel like our lives are extra difficult. It can feel like everyone, except us, was given a handbook for how to live a happy life, but we somehow missed the memo. When we get trapped in the negative cycle of thinking, we are essentially willing all of that 'bad' into existence.

Something always goes wrong. This probably feels like a very familiar thought. Just when things look like they might be getting better, something else happens. You just can't seem to catch a break! By following that winding mental path, we are focusing on the negative. When we focus on only the negative things, we are the reason that the negativity continues.

When our thoughts are positive, and we truly believe in what we are saying and thinking, then our reality becomes that.

Using Affirmations

The use of affirmations can be different from person to person. Some people take a strict approach to it, feeling that they need to say specific phrases 10 times in front of a mirror, or other varying strict methods. Others prefer to write down positive phrases onto sticky notes and post them wherever they will see them often. On the other hand, some people believe it's perfectly acceptable to just use whatever positive phrase comes to mind at that moment, training them to be more mindful.

Not everyone believes in the use of affirmations, and that is perfectly fine! Using positive affirmations is not "mission critical." It is simply an extra tool that is at your disposal for creating the reality that you want to be in. There are other more tangible, or more logic-based, methods of improving self-confidence. There are also plenty of people who like to take a combined approach to things. In this way, they rely on science or medicine, while also using positive affirmations to aid them.

It is up to you to decide which avenue is best for you.

Chapter 9: To a Better You—Positive Affirmations

"Throw yourself into the unknown with pace and a fury defiant. Clothe yourself in beauty untold, and see life as a means to a triumph."
—"Achilles Come Down" by Gang of Youths

Here are a few basic examples of positive affirmations that you can use. However, absolutely feel free to change the wording so that it aligns with whatever situation you are dealing with. Tailor the affirmations to what you need should you choose to utilize them. Please remember: When using positive affirmations to change your reality and boost your self-esteem, really try to work on believing the words and believing that your words and thoughts do have power.

- I deserve happiness.

You do. Everyone deserves to be happy. Happy people live longer and have more peace. Imagine what humans could be capable of if love and happiness ruled them.

- I have value.

We all have value far beyond what we see. There is not a single person alive that does not have value. Not being able to see it yet does not mean it is not there.

- I do not have to be perfect.

Nobody is perfect! The idea of perfection is not at all realistic because perfection does not truly exist. By trying to be perfect, you are only setting yourself up for failure by having something utterly unattainable as your goal.

- This situation is temporary.

The changing of the seasons shows through in the rest of life, as well. Nothing is permanent. As we go through life, it is inevitable to have periods of time–moments, days, or even months–where things seem to go incredibly well, and other periods of time where it feels like nothing is going right. Learn to accept the natural ebb and flow of your own circumstances, and life will feel a little bit less like an unpredictable rollercoaster.

● I live in harmony with myself.

Learning to live in harmony with yourself, rather than be in a constant state of fighting who you are, can feel amazing. Let yourself have that.

● I have the strength to tackle any obstacle.

Look at how much you have done! Take a look at everything you have gone through and survived. You came out on top of it all. It's time to dust off and keep going because that strength is still very much inside you.

● I accept and love myself.

Loving yourself can be one of the hardest lessons to learn, especially if you have been through a lot. However, fewer things bring a boost of happiness and confidence like the one that comes from truly accepting and loving yourself for who you are.

● I allow myself the opportunity to relax and recharge.

If you don't take care of yourself, how are you going to take care of anyone or anything else? Everything that exists needs a break. If you do not allow yourself to relax, you stay stressed and that keeps your mind and body in that survival mode. Allow yourself a chance to relax, you've been working hard to make it through everything.

● Everything is working out for the best in my life.

Trust the process and trust the cycle. You are working on making some great changes to your life and developing the higher self-esteem that you deserve. Things can and do turn around.

● I attract positive energy to myself.

When you truly believe that you are a magnet for positive energy, you become one. By attracting a portion of the positive energy that humanity, and the universe holds, you can replace the negativity with it.

● I am a priority.

You are a priority, we all are. Your happiness matters, you matter. Your life has value. Allow yourself to see that you deserve to treat yourself as a priority in your own life.

● I am worthy of a good life.

We all deserve to have a good life. Certain things in life should come guaranteed: health, happiness, wisdom, and comfort. Wanting a good life is not a bad thing. Regardless of what you may have been told in the past, or what you have believed about yourself, you are worthy of a good life, as well.

● I am heard and respected.

It certainly does not feel that way at times. There are people in your life that make you feel completely alone or worthless. However, some people love and care for you and respect you for who you are. Remind yourself of this.

● I am grateful for the good things in my life.

There is always something in life to be grateful for, we just don't always see it. Think back on your day, or your week. What was just one thing that happened that you are grateful for? Who in your life are you grateful to have there?

● I am an inspiration.

The fact that you have survived everything that you have and you have not let it break you completely is something to be proud of. That kind of strength inspires people to remember how strong they can be, too.

● I am amazing just being myself.

Why would you want to hold yourself to unrealistically high standards, when you are already so amazing? By being authentically you, there are people who are absolutely dazzled by you.

● I am growing more confident every day.

Confidence and self-esteem are like muscles; the more you practice using them, the stronger they will be. Allow yourself to feel better and do better.

● I am confident in my decisions.

Making decisions can be hard, no matter who you are. However, you made the decision for a reason. You are doing the best that you can with what you know and have at the time. Don't look back and tell yourself how you should have done things differently. Try to realize that it was the best decision for you at that moment, and learn from it.

● I am no longer going to criticize myself.

Self-criticism has a time and a place. Giving yourself constructive feedback on how to do things better next time is invaluable. However, practice this with caution at first. If you slip into negative self-talk and it becomes unhelpful critiques, take a mental step back and reassess the situation to give yourself a minute to breathe and center.

● I am living in the now.

Being mindful of the present goes a long way towards a happier and more confident version of you. Deal with tomorrow's problems when tomorrow comes. Let yourself be who you are right here and now. Shifting the focus to the past will not change anything, and shifting the focus to the future brings us unnecessary stress because we can't do anything about it yet. Focus on the now.

Why It Does Not Always Work

Some people believe that using positive affirmations is too good to be true and that it can't be that simple. In a sense, they are correct because there is a small catch. It doesn't matter how many times you repeat an affirmation if you do not believe the words and you don't take any action towards it. You have to put in the work. Positive affirmations can bring you more confidence and motivation to tackle these obstacles, but you still have to put in some effort. Affirmations give you a solid starting point for making the changes.

When we use affirmations and imagine ourselves successfully getting through whatever situation we are in, an interesting thing happens in the brain. Our brains sometimes have a hard time differentiating between reality and what is only our imagination. However, this can be useful!

Imagining yourself getting the job you want helps to activate the same parts of the brain that would be activating if you got the job in your real life. It is the same reaction, physiologically. This can get you into the right mindset to make this happen.

If you find that using affirmations does not work for you or makes you feel worse, then don't use them! They do have some science behind them, but this isn't a one-size-fits-all solution. Use some of the other tips in this book, instead.

Chapter 10: Self-Esteem Building Activities Promoting Self-Love and Acceptance

"Till the roof comes off, 'till the lights go out, 'till my legs give out, can't shut my mouth, 'till the smoke clears out, am I high? Perhaps. I'ma rip this shit, 'till my bone collapse." —"Till I Collapse" by Eminem ft. Nate Dogg

Despite Eminem not being known for his motivational lyrics, the song "Till I Collapse" is a culmination of his lyrical mastery and the kind of "tough love" inspiration that many would be inclined to follow. It is hard-hitting and a realistic reminder that while you may be down and out, it is not the ending chapter of your story; instead, make it your origin story of greatness. The song reminds us that even when we feel weak and feel like we are about to fall flat on our faces, we can still find that quiet, inner strength. You can still see that motivational push within you to not give up or surrender.

We can become the main character of our narrative.

We've established the ideology of low self-esteem and its implications. In previous chapters, we've discussed positive affirmations, then myriads of examples and indications associated with positive affirmations, and a step-by-step method of overcoming low self-esteem.

Now that all of these instances have been discussed, examined, and explained, the very next step is to provide more tangible alternatives to aid in promoting self-love, validation, and acceptance among those suffering from different aspects of low self-esteem. "Tangible' refers to the options that require less emotional bonds and severing and are instead objectives focused on appealing to our need for visual aid.

At times, words of affirmation may have the opposite result despite the good intentions. Some view affirmations as empty platitudes and as a ridiculous subscription to spiritualism and all its falsity. Others may read the steps provided prior and think these steps could potentially be too difficult a task for them to accomplish. If you fall between these two opinions on this imagined spectrum, please note that such a thought process is perfectly reasonable and that your perspectives and viewpoints are always valid.

This chapter intends to give you, the reader, the option to choose alternatives that are not as daunting as a predetermined method of overcoming low self-esteem or as potentially skeptical a concept that repeating positive affirmations as a mantra tends to be. These alternatives are a little lower in the commitment department but are still invaluable in combating or reducing instances of low self-esteem. You can try a mixture of all or some of the presented methods or select the one you are most comfortable with; the choice is ultimately yours. Finding an approach that suits you is the best possible outcome for any scenario. With that prompt, let's examine some activities that can aid in building and promoting self-esteem, love, and confidence.

Dear Me

Sometimes the best person to talk to is yourself, the person looking back at you when you stare in the mirror. "Dear Me" is a writing exercise that prompts you to look inwardly, focusing on all aspects of your psyche.

What you'll need:

- Writing apparatus of any kind—a pen, marker pencil; ultimately, it is your preferred choice that matters!

- Paper of any kind

- An alternative is using a typing application on your device: You can choose Microsoft Word, Google Docs, or any Note-centric app on your phone, tablet, or laptop if you would rather have a more digital trace and organization.

- If you opt for pen and paper, you can use a folder or any appropriate filing item to squirrel away your letters meant for yourself.

Time for the Activity: Unlimited.

For this activity, there are no time constraints. There are instances when it takes quite a long time to organize your thoughts to make any semblance of coherency. Sensory overloading can affect how many words you can jot down at any given time, as all the emotions can become excessive and overwhelming. Take as long as you need to collect yourself and your feelings.

The concept surrounding this activity is to write a letter to yourself. You can determine how frequently you would do so, but the suggestion is to address yourself at least every month. The frequency can increase as you see fit or whenever you feel more comfortable for increasing intimate contact with your emotions and thoughts.

As such, "Dear Me" is an activity that allows you to face your thought both intrusive and cheerful, at your own pace. You can scribble down your deepest fears and times of celebration, addressing these words to yourself. It prompts a deeper understanding of your subconsciousness, giving insights into what can be the root cause of your frustrations, fears, and self-consciousness.

You are in charge of what thoughts you want to address to yourself; there is no wrong or right way of completing this activity. However, you can opt to follow this strategy of writing to yourself as a guide to soothe any sense of indecision or confusion that may occur.

Writing the Letter: A Mini-Guide

Here is a mini guide to crafting multiple letters for yourself. Mix, match, and shift the steps to whichever order of procedure makes you the most comfortable. That is an option if you want to get the most challenging aspects out first. Be mindful of potential triggers, and remember to quit when the emotions become too overwhelming. None of these steps are quick fixes that guarantee rapid results; healing from mental trauma is a steady and often gradual process that is not to be rushed and treated with the utmost seriousness.

1. **Confronting your negative emotions**: This letter focuses on writing any thoughts that are harmful to your mental health, intrusive thoughts, or any associations that can stir up adverse emotions. Please note that this can dredge up memories that you would prefer to leave behind, so only do so when you feel you are suitably ready to face these sentiments or when you have a stable support system that can assist in resurfacing you from those ideas. If you believe you are vulnerable to falling back into patterns of self-hatred, deprecation, or pity if you start using this step first, please move on to the other steps listed below or another method. You are the best judge of your capacity and limits; knowing these hallmarks is essential for persons starting the admittedly daunting journey of rediscovering themselves. Take as long as you need to navigate these emotions, and write them as you see fit. Coherency here is unnecessary; you can write these letters in a stream-of-consciousness style. Let your feelings flow whichever way you are most comfortable and where you feel you have the most control over them.

2. **Highlighting the 'okays'**: "Way Less Sad" by the American band AJR puts this concept in perfect focus with the lyrics, "Livin' sucks, but it's suckin' just a little now" (AJR, 2021). For this letter, there can be multiple letters, you decide! You can focus on the circumstances within your life that you deem to be 'okay'; things that are not overwhelmingly horrible nor are they blissfully spectacular. Doing so can help you realize that while your life may not be the best, you can

find situations where everything turned out okay. Such actualizations can even allow you to find the silver linings where you could only see the worst.

3. **Celebrate your small victories:** No matter how small the achievement is, you can write about it! It could be that you ate healthier or feel a little less sad; all of these instances are causes for celebration. Small steps can cause large ripples of change. Encouraging yourself as you make tiny improvements in your life is a step in the right direction of accepting the person you see in the mirror's reflection.

4. **Who are you?:** It is quite an existential question, but it is apt for the topic. Focus your letters on rediscovering who you are. The letter can include your expected reactions to a particular instance or issue. For example, what would be your immediate reaction to being blamed for something you had zero involvement with? Is your first reaction anger? Resentment? Misplaced guilt? Such reflections on your personality and all its associations can assist in tracing out the outlines of who you are and acknowledging and accepting the person you have written about: *you.*

5. **Loving yourself:** For this step, the intention is to concentrate on the aspects of yourself that you love. It does not have to be a physical feature. The part of yourself you love can be a talent you possess. It can be a part of your personality that you believe is worth admiring. Listing these out can improve your feelings of appreciation for the person you are, despite and because of your scars, wounds, edges, and curves.

The objective of consistently writing to yourself is to gradually move you away from the preconceived prejudices formed against yourself and morph these assertions into acceptance, love, and gratefulness for the person you can become. Your writing ability is not a determinant of your letter and its contents. Remember that these words are for you to grow deeper in love with yourself. You should only show your letter to someone else under the premise that you are sure that the person reading all the thoughts you had never bothered to speak out loud is someone you have utmost faith and trust in.

The book *9 Self-Confidence Building Activities for Students* suggests writing letters to your future and past self, focusing on what you would do going forward and how you remedy your past mistakes, respectively (Cullins, 2021).

Envisioning

Not everyone was gifted the talent of self-expression with diction and how to put the proverbial pen-to-paper required for "Dear Me"; this can cause the activity to be akin to a lofty mountain to ascend. Conversely, trying to sort out your emotions and relieving those thoughts could potentially undo any bits of progress that you have made before this. Despite this, there are still avenues to explore and choose from. Whether you are more in tune with the right-hand side of your brain—the area for the imaginative and innovative thinker—and inclined to focus on aesthetics and its appeals, or if the thought of writing down your thoughts seems to be an endlessly discomforting task, the activity 'envisioning' is perfect for you.

Envisioning is an engaging activity that caters more to the visual reader or those who would find it hard to relive particular moments of frustration and pain and may not be willing to regurgitate their thoughts onto paper. The objective for this activity and its premise is pretty simple: Envisioning is centered around creating a vision board that can aid in creating smaller goals and objectives to become a better version of yourself. Envisioning does this by cataloging and compartmentalizing your goals and aspirations. Doing so can enable you to understand better who you are, serve as a visual reminder of what you can and want to accomplish, and can additionally ascertain your perceptions of your "true self." Envisioning has two potential media: You can complete it through the traditional art media, or you can use a very convenient medium known as Pinterest to collage your expectations digitally.

What you'll need:

- Any available sized paper—the type is wholly optional—and you can make it to your preferred size.

- Colored papers (optional).

- Pictures of the goals you have in mind; you can make the imagery as vague or detailed as you want.

● Colored markers, paint, brushes, or glitter of any variety and color you want; go wild! It is your vision, so embellish it to your heart's content.

Time Limit: No time constraints.

You can make this vision board during your downtime or any available time. Vision boards can be time-consuming and detail-oriented. The construction times vary among individuals. Take as much time as you need, and you can add more images or remove them at any time as your goals and inspirations may change frequently.

If you opt to use Pinterest, you can find the steps to creating a digital vision board below.

Actualizing Your Visions

If you are unfamiliar with the concept, a vision board is a collage of images representing one's goals and dreams (Earley, 2021). It can include cut-outs from magazines, printed images on the internet, or words that inspire and motivate you to manifest your aspirations and the journey you want to chart. A vision board is an excellent means of categorizing and clarifying the goals and aspirations into a visually and aesthetically pleasing motif, especially for you.

So, how do you create one? The creative process is largely up to you: You have the creative liberty to envision what you want on your vision board, but you can follow these steps for a broad idea of how to make one.

1. **Set out your goals and aspirations:** Before you begin the creative process of the vision board, you decide what goals and aspirations you want to highlight. Organizations such as the U.S. Small Business Administration (SBA) and the Federal Deposit Insurance Corporation suggest the *ABC of Priority Tasking* in prioritizing your objectives (Federal Deposit Insurance Corporation & U.S. Small Business Administration, 2016). The ABC method ranks each task with the letter A, B, or C. Some analysts suggest reallocating the 'B' tasks to either 'A" or 'C.' In this case, the objectives you would compile and rank your goals and aspirations, depending on your perceptions and beliefs as that would necessitate the highest priority. Once you have narrowed these down, you can move on to the next step.

2. **Building a vision board:** You will get all your materials here, including your pictures and writing materials. The specific arrangement is up to you, and you can intersperse blank spaces with motivational quotes or keywords to remember. To avoid empty spaces, you can fill these in with overlapping images or random doodles for a bit of fun. Before gluing the pictures down, do a quick layout and positioning of your materials to create a general concept for your vision board. If you are the spontaneous type, you can proceed to create your vision board as is. You can attach anything on the board: mementos, song lyrics, ribbons, or buttons. Make it as uniquely you as

possible, and craft your concept of what your aspirations should be.

You can view a tutorial by Nicole Etolen for a better visual guide on creating a vision board on Teen Entertainment Guide (Etolen, 2015). It breaks down the concept into more understandable illustrations and has photos of the finished product.

You can place your vision board where you can access and notice it effortlessly, as a reminder of what they are working towards, such as on your bedroom wall or just above your work or study desk. The objective of the vision board is to look up at the vision board and be reminded of your goals and aspirations, no matter how small they may seem to others, and to find the motivation to accomplish said dreams.

If you are not the best with your hands, there is a digital alternative: using Pinterest. Pinterest is a social media network and a "visual discovery engine for finding ideas like recipes, home and style inspiration, and more" (Pinterest, 2020). It involves sourcing pictures on the website, or application, and 'pinning' photos that garner your attention. By using Pinterest, you can create a digital copy of your vision and have it saved to the device. There are no additional steps for this option; you can complete it in a few clicks.

Pen-to-Paper

In the age of technology and quick accessibility, the concept of writing contends with considerable reluctance. While it may seem a bit traditional, some may even view it as archaic, journaling can be an excellent means of tracking your thoughts and detailing your expectations. Tracking your ideals and goals can be a healthy measuring stick to gauge your current mental health and the steps to take to address potential warning signs. For this method, it is a little less demanding, material-wise, but can be just as efficient and effective as the other two methods.

So, how does journaling help? Journaling is an essential step for anyone seeking to overcome their issues of low self-esteem or to aid in rebuilding it in the process. Journaling serves as a coping mechanism that provides an avenue for releasing emotions without the added pressure of relaying them to others (Fish, 2020).

An article, "Journal Prompts for Mental Health & More on Journaling!", emphasizes that journaling and detailing your emotions and thought process can aid in identifying patterns of 'spirals' or potential triggers unique to your situation. Such practices are discernable when we document and note troubles and ordeals that increase our likelihood of falling into destructive thoughts and habits and pinpointing what or who had prompted such an event.

The concept of journaling can be a method of organizing your thoughts and compartmentalizing them so that you are not wholly overwhelmed by instances occurring in your life. As such, developing a mini-routine of checking in on yourself by writing a journal can become beneficial as taking a few minutes out of your time to write a bit can do wonders for increasing your confidence—and, by extension, your self-esteem—as it allows for a sort of soothing routine to fall into. Routines and habits are not necessarily harmful concepts and are only dangerous when we become so set within them that we lose sight of everything else around us.

Where the words may fail you, you can write them out instead.

You do not have to create any journal to do this. Just use pre-made bullet journals or planners or even use your electronic devices to track your development and correspondence with yourself. All creative liberty is up to your discretion; you can detail and write as you see fit without restrictions. Zapier.com curated a top listing for the best apps to use on your journaling journey, along with their most compatible operating system (Pot, 2022):

- Day One: compatible with Mac, iOS, watchOS, and Android
- Diarium: compatible with Windows, Android, macOS, and iOS
- Penzu: compatible with Web, iOS, and Android
- Momento: compatible with iOS
- Grid Diary: compatible with macOS, Android, and iOS
- Five Minute Journal: compatible with iOS and Android
- Dabble Me: consistent with the Web
- Daylio: compatible with iOS and Android

Fish has listed some excellent prompts for starting your journaling in their post, *Journal Prompts for Mental Health & More on Journaling!* in a bid to assist their readers in the goals of establishing who they are and as a measure of tracking and observing where they were previously, and where they are now (Fish, 2020). Here are a few select ones:

1. What does a perfect day look like to you?
2. Identify three short-term goals and one long-term goal. Try to elaborate on how you would achieve these goals.
3. Why am I Happy Today? List a collectively growing list of why you are happy. Work upwards from one to an unlimited number of reasons.
4. Write down three to five things that trigger feelings of anxiety in you, but be mindful of triggering potential traumas and harmful memories. Attempt to identify at least one coping strategy to respond to these triggers.
5. What things are you avoiding confrontation about? List at least three.

None of these methods is a fool-proof solution. It is a herculean task to find a panacea for any problem, but they are still necessary for building self-esteem. Focusing on any of these methods can aid in finding self-love as they can help discover previously hidden aspects of yourself, which fosters a spirit of acceptance and love for yourself.

One Small Step at a Time

In everything we do, especially on a journey for better mental health and higher levels of self-esteem, taking one step at a time is invaluable and fundamental advice. Forcing a situation to progress faster than we are mentally capable or ready for often has irreparable damage and causes setbacks for our transitional healing period.

It is imperative that, regardless of your preferred method you will use on your journey, take everything in small strides. Work your way up in small increments, and you will be surprised at how much growth you can accomplish by making small but impactful changes.

Jamaicans have this saying: One coco full basket, with the translation equating to gathering one coco at a time, will fill the basket. In other words, the road to success has no shortcuts, and it is a step-by-step process; by taking our time and rediscovering ourselves in the process, we will eventually become the person written among the stars and reach that point where we can stand proud of ourselves, and to feel nothing but positive emotions and love towards the inner person (Loop News, 2016; Staff Writer (Anon.), 2012).

Overcoming low self-esteem is not a one-time "fixer-upper"; it is a continuous cycle, and it is thus essential to take one step at a time, despite how difficult that first step may seem.

Therapy

If you are the type to dive into Quora and Reddit quickly, once you come across a question you can't seem to get answered–as is the current predilection– you'll find many opinions and concerns when people ask about the effectiveness of therapy. For all it is worth and the stigma that surrounds it at times, therapy can be a valuable means of overcoming low self-esteem issues. Defined as a comprehensive terminology-based treatment system that uses psychology-based methods to assist and treat persons with various mental disorders (Saybrook University, 2020), therapy is a step in the right direction when overcoming low self-esteem. Licensed and professionally trained therapists can provide consistent and crucial assistance that can assist persons seeking to build the best possible version of themselves. Tina Gilbertson, MA, LPC puts this concept to the test in her article, "Does Therapy for Low Self-Esteem Really Work?" (Gilbertson, MA, LPC, 2016):

> Therapy creates an experience of being basically acceptable instead of basically wrong, and this naturally improves self-esteem. By treating you as acceptable, the therapist models a different way for you to relate to yourself.

BACP (UK) further elaborates on this thought process. The organization's page, in collaboration with counselor Natasha Page, states that therapy and counseling aid in the exploration and analysis of the internal mechanism within the subconscious mind; the overall concept and purpose of therapy is to use the results of the mental investigation and to change thus the person's perception and potentially biased opinions of themselves and others (BACP & Page, 2019). "Counselling Directory" identifies that a counselor can aid the process of triumphing over low self-esteem as they assist in finding out the root causes of your self-perception and the best methods to combat and challenge these often incorrect and limiting belief systems (Gifford, 2022).

There are different approaches that therapists may implement during treatment; each method is unique and is not guaranteed to work on an individual basis (Psychologen Amsterdam, 2020). Here are a few types used by therapists:

1. Cognitive-behavioral therapy (CBT): is psychotherapy that combines cognitive therapy with behavior therapy by identifying faulty or maladaptive patterns of thinking, emotional response, or behavior and substituting them with desirable ways of thinking, emotional response, or behavior (Merriam-Webster, 1818b).
2. Eye Movement Desensitization and Reprocessing Therapy (EMDR): specifically used if low self-esteem issues stem from trauma, EMDR is defined–by the EMDR Institute–as such:

[A method of] psychotherapy that enables people to heal from the symptoms and emotional distress that are the result of disturbing life experiences... EMDR therapy shows that the mind can in fact heal from psychological trauma much as the body recovers from physical trauma... Using the detailed protocols and procedures learned in EMDR therapy training sessions, clinicians help clients activate their natural healing processes.

1. Acceptance and Commitment Therapy (ACT): The patient is encouraged to accept negative thoughts and emotions as a part of normal psychological functioning and to commit to action based on the patient's values and goals (Merriam-Webster, 1818a).

However, it is essential to note that therapy is not without its limitations, especially in light of the clashing personality traits and more *judgment* and less *compassion*–not pity, which is expressly different from the connotative and denotative nature of 'compassion'–from the therapist's end. Instances of an increase in anxiety levels have been observed through the interactions between therapist and patient but are mainly on the occasions in which the therapist may have conflicts of interest as well. (Linden & Schermuly-Haupt, 2014).

In the age of immediate satisfaction and ease of social media accessibility, online therapists have become rife and proliferated across various social media sites or mental health content creators. Each person may diagnose their peers by using similar symptoms to assign persons with mental disorders or illnesses, with–on occasion–the same symptoms being given to an entirely different complication by different content creators. It is a dangerous habit that is not free of its various implications. There is nothing inherently wrong with well-intentioned persons seeking to educate about the impact of mental health; however, it may cause unforeseen issues, such as oversimplifying mental complications, allowing persons to misdiagnose their mental health issues, or addressing the complexity behind the whys and not the solution. *Do #MentalHealth TikToks Help or Hurt? A Therapist Breaks It Down* by WebMD puts this concept in a perfect summary (Nazario, MD, 2022):

> The [TikTok] algorithm can be damaging to people with anxieties who may find their fears worsened by the videos on their feeds. Similarly, TikTok content seems hung up on diagnoses and symptoms. It's easy to see videos talking about relatable symptoms and thinking, "Hey, that's me."

It is best to do research to find the best therapist to cater to your unique circumstances and not to limit yourself to what you may see on the internet; finding the right therapist and sticking to their outlined plans can be worthwhile and indispensable to reducing low self-esteem and promoting feelings of self-love and positivity.

Healthy Eating

Surprisingly, healthy eating can promote confidence and acceptance of ourselves. The saying, and not the television program, "You are what you eat" may perpetuate certain unhealthy assumptions and ramifications, but it does have a large nugget of knowledge between the words: what we eat often plays an impactful role in our moods and our perceived biases aimed towards to ourselves and others. At times, our spirit also depends on what we have eaten previously. Jo Withers, a registered dietitian, notes this in her article, "Mindful eating—finding ways to be kinder to yourself," which puts this ideology into perspective (Withers, 2016):

> When we are eating out of synchronization with our bodies, some people find that feelings of guilt and shame follow and this self-judgment cycle can lead to food restriction, overeating, or yo-yo dieting which have shown to have a negative impact on well-being and health outcomes.

Our unhealthy relationship with our eating habits and tendencies can be the proverbial deal-breaker that influences the resulting self-esteem and confidence. However, you may wonder how eating healthily may improve your mood and, by extension, your esteem. It is pretty simple: serotonin is derived chiefly from your gut rather than your brain.

According to an article by the Cleveland Clinic, 90% of the total serotonin produced is "found in the cells lining your gastrointestinal tract. Only about 10% is produced in your brain" (Cleveland Clinic, 2022). Bamalan and Al Khalili define serotonin, or 5-hydroxytryptamine (5-HT), as a "neurotransmitter of an integral physiological role in the human body; it is involved in the regulation of various activities [such as] behavior, mood, and memory" (Bamalan & Al Khalili 2020). Serotonin consists of the essential amino acid tryptophan, an essential element that cannot be produced by the body naturally. Instead, we obtained it from eaten foods (Cleveland Clinic, 2022). Essentially, it is a transmitter that allows for feelings of happiness to be spread within the body, improving one's physical and mental states, and promoting a better standard of health. Thus, an unhealthy diet can truncate gut health, reducing the amount of serotonin produced by the body as your brain can only generate a small quantity in comparison.

Substituting more processed foods for healthier alternatives can significantly change your health; for example, switching out that donut you grabbed at breakfast for some fruits and yogurt. Mix it up a bit with some nuts thrown in as well. The fast-moving pace of contemporary society is inclined to quick options to help keep you moving and awake enough to be considered active but does not foster nutritious eating. In the article, "Confidence and self-esteem," Katherine Nicholls relays foods that promote healthier eating practices and improve your mood, perception of yourself, and ultimately your esteem (Nicholls, 2019). She emphasizes the increased intake of foods rich in the following nutrients:

- Carbohydrates and protein: focus more on unrefined carbohydrates–i.e., minimally processed or 'whole'– foods, such as whole grains, fruits, vegetables, and beans. For protein, excellent sources include meat, fish, eggs, and pulses.

- Omega-3 fatty acids: omega-3 fatty acids are excellent boosts for neurotransmitters and are abundant in oily fishes such as sardines and mackerel.

- Vitamin D, B, and selenium: foods rich in these nutrients are essential for promoting serotonin levels and can be found in nuts, beans, eggs, fish, vegetables, and other similar food types.

However, due to the particularities of medical history and potential food allergies, you must always consult your doctor before attempting to change any aspects of your diet, no matter how small the change may be. Your health is of utmost importance and knowing your limits, exceptions, and allowances is a vital first step.

Exercising

As daunting a scenario as both aspects often appear, exercising and socializing help increase your self-esteem and confidence. Fernández-Bustos et al. (2019), in their research article "Effect of Physical Activity on Self-Concept: Theoretical Model on the Mediation of Body Image and Physical Self-Concept in Adolescents," state that a study of 652 Spanish students, ages 12-17, concludes that the implementation of physical activity in the student's lifestyles comprehensively aided them to achieve a greater sense of positive self-esteem through the increased positive perceptions associated with boy image and satisfaction. Such a study is not limited to only younger persons; persons within all demographics can benefit from interspersing aspects of physical activity into their daily routine.

To further this concept, Sani et al. proposed an analytic study focused on the correlation between self-esteem, body image, and physical activity (or exercising), hypothesizing different possibilities and causative lines (Sani et al., 2016). The study hypothesizes that the participants who reported higher levels of physical activity engagement would experience higher levels of self-esteem and that persons who engage more in physical activity are inclined to have a more positive body image. Butterfly Foundation defines "body image" as the culmination of the thoughts, perceived imagery, and perceptions in correlation to our bodies and includes our view of our shapes, sizes, gender identities, et cetera (The Butterfly Foundation, 2021). Their research confirmed that physical activities directly correlated with self-esteem, stemming from indirect factors such as body mass index (BMI) and body image.

So what does this mean for you?

"Exercise for Mental Health" elaborates that exercising can improve mental health as it aids in the reduction of anxiety and depressive moods and increases self-esteem and cognitive functions (Sharma et al., 2006). Additionally, while healthy eating promotes serotonin, exercising induces increased amounts of endorphins in the body. According to Harvard Health, endorphin–coined from the term "endogenous morphine"–is the brain's natural pain reliever and is a chemical hormone released in response to pain or stress (Harvard Health Publishing, 2021). In other words, endorphins are "feel good" hormones released when we laugh, fall in love, or eat a delicious meal. Exercising is one of the best ways to promote these happy feelings within your body. As it is endogenous, endorphins are not reliant on external factors but already exist within our bodies, thus meaning that we are the ones in charge of spreading those good vibes within ourselves.

Simply put, exercising can be an excellent means of promoting self-esteem with endless opportunities and avenues to explore for a better version of yourself. Running and other sports-related activities are just the tip of the proverbial iceberg. You can try taking up dancing, rowing, or fencing; the possibilities are yours for the taking. Even walking for a few minutes can be a great way to clear up the thoughts running through your head and aids in focusing on the bigger picture rather than being swallowed up by the details in the smaller one.

Conclusion

Throughout these chapters, there are snippets of wisdom from many people who have been exactly where you are; needing a change, and unsure where to start.

This book has given you many techniques and ideas for how you can help yourself shape the life and reality that you want and deserve. If you are ready for change, then do it. You, and you alone, are in control of your life. Take what works for you, leave behind the rest, and give yourself the life that you deserve. Listen to the songs listed in many of the chapters and keep what resonates with you.

Always remember: You are not alone, and you are stronger than you realize.

Glossary

- Attribute (noun): quality, character, or characteristic ascribed to someone or something; an object closely associated with or belonging to a specific person, thing, or office

○ Attribute (verb): to explain (something) by indicating a cause; to regard as a characteristic of a person or thing; to reckon as made or originated in a predicted fashion

- Body dysmorphia (medical dictionary): the pathological preoccupation with an imagined or slight physical defect of one's body to the point of causing significant stress or behavioral impairment in several areas (as work and personal relationships)

- Deprecate (transitive verb): to express disapproval of; play down–to make little of; belittle, disparage

- Esteem (noun): the regard in which one is held

○ Esteem (verb): to set a high value on regard highly and prize accordingly

- Identity (noun): the distinguishing character or personality of an individual; the concept of individuality

○ See also identification (noun): psychological orientation of the self regarding something (such as a person or group) with a resulting feeling of close emotional association; a largely unconscious process whereby an individual models thoughts, feelings, and actions after those attributed to an object that has been incorporated as a mental image

- Idiosyncrasy (noun): a peculiarity of constitution or temperament: an individualizing characteristic or quality

● Reflexive (noun) (about psychology): directed or turned back on itself; of, relating to, characterized by, or being a relation that exists between an entity and itself; of, relating to, or constituting an action directed back on the agent or the grammatical subject

● Self-Attribution (noun): refers to individuals' tendency to attribute successes to personal skills and failures to factors beyond their control

● Self-Awareness (noun): an awareness of one's own personality or individuality

● Self-Esteem (noun): confidence and satisfaction in oneself; self-respect; self-conceit

● Self-Reference (noun): the act or an instance of referring or alluding to oneself or itself

● Self (noun): an individual's typical character or behavior; the union of elements (such as body, emotions, thoughts, and sensations) that constitute the individuality and identity of a person

○ Self (adjective) having a single character or quality throughout

● Self-esteem (noun): confidence and satisfaction in oneself; conceit

● Subconscious (adjective): existing in mind but not immediately available to consciousness

○ Subconscious): the mental activities just below the threshold of consciousness (n

References

8 Common Examples of Low Self-Esteem. (2021, August 3). Psych Central. https://psychcentral.com/health/common-patterns-of-low-self-esteem

Admin. (2018, January 30). *4 Benefits of Positive Affirmations.* HeadWay Clinic. https://www.headwayclinic.ca/4-benefits-positive-affirmations/

Affirmations: What Are They and How Do They Work? (n.d.). Www.familycentre.org. Retrieved August 26, 2022, from https://www.familycentre.org/news/post/affirmations-what-are-they-and-how-do-they-work

Alton, L. (2017, November 15). *Why low self-esteem may be hurting you at work.* NBC News; NBC News. https://www.nbcnews.com/better/business/why-low-self-esteem-may-be-hurting-your-career-ncna814156

Alves, R. (2017, July 25). *What Factors Influence Your Self-esteem?* Essence of Healing Counseling. https://www.essenceofhealingcounseling.com/what-factors-influence-your-self-esteem/

Antonucci, T. C., & Jackson, J. S. (1983). Physical health and self-esteem. *Family and Community Health*, 6(2), 1–9. https://www.jstor.org/stable/44952607

Auld, S. (2019, November 4). *Social media and low self-esteem.* ACC Blog. https://www.acc.edu.au/blog/social-media-low-self-esteem/

Bardo, N. (2021, July 30). *20 Confidence Building Exercises and Self-Esteem Activities.* It's All You Boo. https://itsallyouboo.com/confidence-building-exercises/

Better Health Channel. (2012). *Self-esteem*. Vic.gov.au. https://www.betterhealth.vic.gov.au/health/healthyliving/self-esteem

Bowden, D. (2018, August 9). *Irreverent Gent*. Irreverent Gent. https://www.irreverentgent.com/social-media-and-self-esteem-statistics/

Calmerry. (2021, September 9). *Crossing the Line: When Self-Deprecation Turns to Self-Hate | Calmerry*. Calmerry Blog. https://us.calmerry.com/blog/self-esteem/what-is-self-deprecation/

Canadian Mental Health Association. (2015). *Body Image, Self-Esteem, and Mental Health | Here to Help*. Heretohelp.bc.ca. https://www.heretohelp.bc.ca/infosheet/body-image-self-esteem-and-mental-health

Chong, C. (2017, March 22). *Signs Of Low Self-Esteem And The Root Causes You Might Not Know*. Lifehack; Lifehack. https://www.lifehack.org/565816/low-self-esteem

Contributor. (2017, August 2). *How To Overcome The 4 Roadblocks To Self-Development*. Young Upstarts. https://www.youngupstarts.com/2017/08/02/how-to-overcome-the-4-roadblocks-to-self-development/

Creatio. (2021, July 2). *The Importance of Affirmations*. The Y. https://www.ymcansw.org.au/news-and-media/the-y-at-home/the-importance-of-affirmations/

doctor.ndtv.com. (2018, May 1). *Warning Signs That A Person Has A Low Self-Esteem*. Doctor.ndtv.com. https://doctor.ndtv.com/living-healthy/warning-signs-that-a-person-has-a-low-self-esteem-1821675

Edmondson, A. (2011, April). *Strategies for Learning from Failure.* Harvard Business Review. https://hbr.org/2011/04/strategies-for-learning-from-failure

Gambini, B. (2017, April 27). *Staking self-worth on the pursuit of money has negative psychological consequences.* Www.buffalo.edu. https://www.buffalo.edu/news/releases/2017/04/046.html

Gertler, B. (2021). *Self-Knowledge > Knowledge of the Self (Stanford Encyclopedia of Philosophy).* Plato.stanford.edu. https://plato.stanford.edu/entries/self-knowledge/supplement.html

Gooden, A. (2020, November 18). *How to cultivate a sense of unconditional self-worth.* Ideas.ted.com. https://ideas.ted.com/how-to-cultivate-a-sense-of-unconditional-self-worth/

Harvey, O. (2017, August 11). *5 concerning things low self esteem can do to your body.* HelloGiggles. https://hellogiggles.com/lifestyle/health-fitness/things-low-self-esteem-does-to-your-body/

HealthDirect. (2019, February 17). *Self-esteem and mental health.* Healthdirect.gov.au; Healthdirect Australia. https://www.healthdirect.gov.au/self-esteem

Henshaw, S. (2014, March 20). *Why Positive Affirmations Don't Work.* Psych Central. https://psychcentral.com/blog/why-positive-affirmations-dont-work#1

Krauss, S., & Orth, U. (n.d.). *Does your work influence your self-esteem and vice versa?* The EJP Blog. Retrieved August 26, 2022, from https://www.ejp-blog.com/blog/2021/7/23/does-your-work-influence-your-self-esteem-and-vice-versa

Krauss, S., & Orth, U. (2021). Work Experiences and Self-Esteem Development: A Meta-Analysis of Longitudinal Studies. *European*

Journal of Personality, 089020702110271. https://doi.org/ 10.1177/08902070211027142

Kristenson, S. (2021, November 23). *60 Affirmations to Boost Your Confidence and Self Esteem.* Happier Human. https://www.happierhuman.com/affirmations-confidence/

Lamia, M. (2010, October 22). *Do Bullies Really Have Low Self-Esteem? | Psychology Today.* Www.psychologytoday.com. https://www.psychologytoday.com/intl/blog/intense-emotions-and-strong-feelings/201010/do-bullies-really-have-low-self-esteem

Leary, M. R. (1999). The social and psychological importance of self-esteem. *The Social Psychology of Emotional and Behavioral Problems: Interfaces of Social and Clinical Psychology.*, 197–221. https://doi.org/10.1037/10320-007

Loades, M. (n.d.). *The overlap between low self-esteem and anxiety/ depression in CAMHS.* ACAMH. https://www.acamh.org/ research-digest/self-esteem-anxiety-depression/

Mayo Clinic. (2020, July 14). *Does your self-esteem need a boost?* Mayo Clinic. https://www.mayoclinic.org/healthy-lifestyle/ adult-health/in-depth/self-esteem/art-20047976

Mayo Clinic Staff. (2017). *7 steps to boost your self-esteem.* Mayo Clinic. https://www.mayoclinic.org/healthy-lifestyle/adult-health/ in-depth/self-esteem/art-20045374

McClure, A. C., Tanski, S. E., Kingsbury, J., Gerrard, M., & Sargent, J. D. (2010). Characteristics Associated With Low Self-Esteem Among US Adolescents. *Academic Pediatrics*, 10(4), 238-244.e2. https://doi.org/10.1016/j.acap.2010.03.007

McGee, R., Williams, S., & Nada-Raja, S. (2001). Low Self-Esteem and Hopelessness in Childhood and Suicidal Ideation in Early

Adulthood. *Journal of Abnormal Child Psychology*, 29(4), 281–291. https://doi.org/10.1023/a:1010353711369

Mind. (2019, January). *About self-esteem*. Mind.org.uk. https://www.mind.org.uk/information-support/types-of-mental-health-problems/self-esteem/about-self-esteem/

Moore, C. (2019, March 4). *Positive Daily Affirmations: Is There Science Behind It?* PositivePsychology.com. https://positivepsychology.com/daily-affirmations/

Morin, A. (2017, July 17). *5 Ways To Turn Your Mistake Into A Valuable Life Lesson*. Forbes. https://www.forbes.com/sites/amymorin/2017/07/17/5-ways-to-turn-your-mistake-into-a-valuable-life-lesson/?sh=4fbf208e1c01

Newman, S. (n.d.). *The Importance of Self-esteem - NIU - Child Development and Family Center*. Northern Illinois University. https://www.chhs.niu.edu/child-center/resources/articles/self-esteem.shtml

NHS. (2021, February 1). *Raising low self-esteem*. Nhs.uk. https://www.nhs.uk/mental-health/self-help/tips-and-support/raise-low-self-esteem/

Overbye, K., Bøen, R., Huster, R. J., & Tamnes, C. K. (2020). Learning From Mistakes: How Does the Brain Handle Errors? *Frontiers for Young Minds*, 8. https://doi.org/10.3389/frym.2020.00080

Pariseau, T. (n.d.). *5 Self-Esteem Activities for Adults That Will Make Your LIFE easier? in Nov 2021 - OurFamilyWorld.com*. Https://Www.ourfamilyworld.com/. https://www.ourfamilyworld.com/family-life/healthy-kids/5-self-esteem-activities-for-adults-that-will-make-your-life-easier/

Powell, K. (2009). The Role of Concept of Self and Societal Expectations in Academic and Career Achievement. *Journal of Adult Education*, *38*(2). https://files.eric.ed.gov/fulltext/EJ891079.pdf

Raypole, C. (2020, September 1). *Do Affirmations Work? Yes, but There's a Catch*. Healthline. https://www.healthline.com/health/mental-health/do-affirmations-work

RefreshMH. (2015, June 23). *Untangling The Links Between Money, Self-Esteem, and Happiness*. Urban Balance. https://www.urbanbalance.com/unearthing-the-link-between-money-self-esteem-and-happiness/

Sasson, R. (2019, March 22). *Are You Repeating Negative Affirmations unintentionally?* Success Consciousness. https://www.successconsciousness.com/blog/affirmations/negative-affirmations/

Sawhney, V. (2020, November 10). *It's Okay to Not Be Okay*. Harvard Business Review. https://hbr.org/2020/11/its-okay-to-not-be-okay

Sowislo, J. F., & Orth, U. (2013). Does low self-esteem predict depression and anxiety? A meta-analysis of longitudinal studies. *Psychological Bulletin*, *139*(1), 213–240. https://doi.org/10.1037/a0028931

Stump, S. (2015, August 3). *Is there a secret bully in all of us? It might be in our genes, study finds*. TODAY.com. https://www.today.com/parents/study-bullies-have-higher-self-esteem-social-status-lower-levels-t36271

Swaddle, T. (2020, January 9). *Low Self-Esteem Can Seep Into Physical Behaviors, Cause Health Issues*. The Swaddle. https://theswaddle.com/self-esteem-physical-effects/

Thompson, A. H. (2010). The Suicidal Process and Self-Esteem. *Crisis, 31*(6), 311–316. https://doi.org/10.1027/0227-5910/a000045

Tips to improve your self-esteem | Mind, the mental health charity - help for mental health problems. (2019). Mind.org.uk. https://www.mind.org.uk/information-support/types-of-mental-health-problems/self-esteem/tips-to-improve-your-self-esteem/

Tirel, M. (2019, July 25). *7 Activities That Will Boost Your Self-Esteem (With Examples).* Tracking Happiness. https://www.trackinghappiness.com/self-esteem-activities/

Tong, E. (2021). *Higher Income Predicts Feelings Such as Pride and Confidence.* Apa.org. https://www.apa.org/news/press/releases/2021/03/higher-income-pride-confidence

Trzesniewski, K. H., Donnellan, M. B., Moffitt, T. E., Robins, R. W., Poulton, R., & Caspi, A. (2006). Low self-esteem during adolescence predicts poor health, criminal behavior, and limited economic prospects during adulthood. *Developmental Psychology, 42*(2), 381–390. https://doi.org/10.1037/0012-1649.42.2.381

Warrell, D. M. (2020, June 5). *Beware Toxic Positivity: It's Okay Not To Feel Okay.* Forbes. https://www.forbes.com/sites/margiewarrell/2020/06/05/had-a-tough-week-sometimes-feeling-bad-is-good-for-you/?sh=64bf23a378d5

Winch, G. (2016, August 23). *5 ways to build lasting self-esteem.* Ideas.ted.com; ideas.ted.com. https://ideas.ted.com/5-ways-to-build-lasting-self-esteem/

Wood, J. V., & Lockwood, P. (1999). Social comparisons in dysphoric and low self-esteem people. *The Social Psychology of Emotional and Behavioral Problems: Interfaces of Social and Clinical Psychology,* 97–135. https://doi.org/10.1037/10320-004

Resources

American Foundation for Suicide Prevention. (2019, February 28). *AFSP*. AFSP. https://afsp.org/

Anxiety and Depression Association of America. (2019). *Understand the Facts | Anxiety and Depression Association of America, ADAA*. Adaa.org. https://adaa.org/understanding-anxiety

Anxiety and Depression Association of America. (2022). *Depression Test*. MHA Screening. https://www.mentalhealthamerica.net/mental-health-screen/patient-health

APA. (2022). *American Psychological Association*. Apa.org. https://www.apa.org/

Care for Your Mind. (2022). *Care for Your Mind*. Care for Your Mind. https://careforyourmind.org/

Crisis Text Line. (2013). *Crisis Text Line*. Crisis Text Line. https://www.crisistextline.org/

Erika's Lighthouse. (2021). *A Beacon of Hope for Adolescent Depression*. Erika's Lighthouse. https://www.erikaslighthouse.org/

Etta. (2008, January). Depression Marathon. *Depression Marathon | Blogger*. https://depressionmarathon.blogspot.com/#axzz55EGd6MGZ2

Medicine Assistance Tool. (n.d.). *Medicine Assistance Tool | MAT.org*. Medicineassistancetool.org. Retrieved June 12, 2022, from https://medicineassistancetool.org/

National Institute of Mental Health (NIMH). (n.d.). *NIMH»
About NIMH*. Www.nimh.nih.gov. Retrieved June 12, 2022, from
https://www.nimh.nih.gov/about

National Suicide Prevention Lifeline. (2019). *National suicide
prevention lifeline*. Suicidepreventionlifeline.org.
https://suicidepreventionlifeline.org/

Substance Abuse and Mental Health Services Administration
(SAMHSA). (2019). *Resources and Programs | Suicide Prevention
Resource Center*. Sprc.org. https://www.sprc.org/resources-programs

The Trevor Project. (1999). *Get Help Now*. The Trevor Project.
https://www.thetrevorproject.org/
get-help-now/#sm.001frwkek412crb10pc21co78w8rc

Therapy for Black Girls. (2022). *Therapy For Black Girls*. Therapy for
Black Girls. https://therapyforblackgirls.com/

Trans Lifeline. (2018). *Trans Lifeline—Peer support services, hotline
and resources for Transgender People Trans Lifeline*. Trans Lifeline.
https://www.translifeline.org/

Don't miss out!

Visit the website below and you can sign up to receive emails whenever DUKE KING publishes a new book. There's no charge and no obligation.

https://books2read.com/r/B-A-FFUW-XHTFC

BOOKS 2 READ

Connecting independent readers to independent writers.

About the Author

Duke King Bursting with an optimistic outlook on life, they have become disheartened by the heavily pessimistic atmosphere that exists in contemporary society, and believe that the right way forward is to provide their readers with informational, and positive reading material. As such, they sought to help those who suffer from low self-esteem and provide invaluable assistance needed to overcome low levels of self-esteem, thus strengthening that sense of self-worth.

Read more at AUTHORDUKEKING.COM.

www.ingramcontent.com/pod-product-compliance
Lightning Source LLC
LaVergne TN
LVHW051124080426
835510LV00018B/2216